REFLECTIVE ENQUIRY
INTO
THERAPEUTIC INSTITUTIONS

THE CASSEL HOSPITAL MONOGRAPH SERIES

1   Psychosocial Practice within a Residential Setting
    edited by Peter Griffiths and Pamela Pringle

THE CASSEL HOSPITAL MONOGRAPH SERIES

REFLECTIVE ENQUIRY INTO THERAPEUTIC INSTITUTIONS

Edited by
Lesley Day & Pamela Pringle

David Bell   *Peter Griffiths*
R. D. Hinshelwood   *Tom Main*
Agata Pisula   *Pamela Pringle*
Wilhelm Skogstad

Foreword by
Kevin Healy

London & New York
KARNAC BOOKS

First published in 2001 by
H. Karnac (Books) Ltd., 6 Pembroke Buildings
London NW10 6RE

A subsidiary of Other Press LLC, New York

British Library Cataloguing in Publication Data

A C.I.P. for this book is available from the British Library

ISBN 1 85575 248 8

10 9 8 7 6 5 4 3 2 1

Edited, designed, and produced by Communication Crafts

Printed and bound in Great Britain by Biddles Ltd, *www.biddles.co.uk*

www.karnacbooks.com

CONTENTS

CONTRIBUTORS

David Bell is a Consultant Psychotherapist and Psychiatrist in the Adult Department of the Tavistock Clinic. Previously, he was Consultant Psychotherapist in the Adult Unit at the Cassel Hospital. He is a member of the British Psycho-Analytical Society.

Lesley Day, BA, MSc (Econ), MSc (Psychotherapy), Dip Integ Psychotherapy, Dip Psy Couns, is Head of the Training and Consultancy Department at the Cassel Hospital and an Adult Psychotherapist in the Outpatient Service and in private practice. Prior to joining the Cassel, she was a Senior Lecturer in Social Science at Brunel University. She has published in the fields of policy, social work, and psychotherapy and is co-editor of *Women, Oppression and Social Work: Issues in Anti-Discriminatory Practice* (Routledge).

Peter Griffiths, BSc, SRN, RMN, Cassel Cert, is Principal Lecturer in Child and Family Health Nursing, a joint post between the Tavistock Clinic and Middlesex University. From 1989 to 1999 he worked at the Cassel Hospital, developing models of psychosocial practice through research, the development of courses within and outside of the Cassel, publication, and training and consultancy in other health care settings. He is currently researching for a PhD at Birkbeck College. He is the co-editor of two books, *Face to Face with*

Distress: The Professional Use of Self in Psychosocial Care (Butter-worth-Heinemann) and *Psychosocial Practice in a Residential Setting* (Karnac Books), and is Deputy Editor of the journal *Therapeutic Communities.*

Kevin Healy is a Consultant Psychotherapist and has been Direc-tor of the Cassel Hospital since 1997. He has worked at the Cassel Hospital since 1986 as a Senior Registrar, Consultant on the in-patient Adult Unit, and latterly as Consultant on the inpatient Adolescent Unit.

Bob Hinshelwood was Clinical Director of the Cassel Hospital from 1993 to 1997. He is now Professor of Psychoanalytic Studies at the University of Essex. He is a member of the British Psycho-Analytical Society. He founded the *International Journal of Therapeu-tic Communities* and the *British Journal of Psychotherapy* and is author of *What Happens in Groups, A Dictionary of Kleinian Thought,* and *Clinical Klein* (Free Association Books) and of *Therapy or Coer-cion: Does Psychotherapy Differ from Brainwashing?* (Karnac Books).

Tom Main was a psychoanalyst and Medical Director of the Cassel Hospital from 1946 to 1976. He was largely responsible for the development of the therapeutic community that was established at the Cassel. He was also President of the Institute of Psychosexual Medicine.

Agata Pisula, BSc, Postgraduate Dip Psychology, RGN, Dip Psy-chosocial Nursing, has worked at the Cassel Hospital for four years. She is currently a senior nurse on the Adult Unit.

Pam Pringle, MSc Interprofessional Health and Welfare Studies, BA (Hons), RGN, RMN, Cassel Cert, has been working as the Outreach/Research Nurse at the Cassel Hospital. She has devel-oped a model of psychosocial practice for patients in the commu-nity. She has recently taken up a Clinical Nurse Specialist post at the Cassel.

Wilhelm Skogstad has been the Consultant Psychotherapist to the Adult Unit of the Cassel Hospital since 1995. He trained in psy-chiatry in Germany and in psychoanalytic psychotherapy and psychoanalysis in Germany, at the Tavistock Clinic, the Cassel Hospital and more recently with the British Psycho-Analytical Society.

FOREWORD

Kevin Healy

This is the second in a series of monographs that aims to provide accessible teaching texts about therapeutic practice in residential settings. The model of practice described is an effective, evidence-based, psychoanalytically informed one that helps disturbed individuals, couples, and families to face change. The first monograph presented the psychosocial model of care that has been developed at the Cassel Hospital over the past fifty years. The monograph illustrated the creative use that can be made of ordinary everyday events and also examined the emotional reactions to the work by staff and the struggle that workers have to understand and make therapeutic use of these feelings. There is a danger, however, in publishing such work: the presentation of a clear and specific model of practice can promote the idea that there is a right way of doing things. Practice developed over time runs the risk of becoming fixed and ritualized, no longer sensitive to the needs of patients.

Life in this therapeutic institution, as elsewhere, involves a constant movement from one state to another. This second monograph demonstrates the need constantly to examine and enquire into practice in order to ensure that it is responsive and dynamic. Developing a culture of enquiry requires dialogue with one's colleagues but also the outside world. Living organisms must communicate with their environment if they are to survive. Institutions are no different: without communication, they too will soon wither and die.

As Director of the Cassel Hospital, I have grappled—as have my predecessors and colleagues—with the non-therapeutic use of knowledge and learning that may serve as a way of avoiding thinking. This monograph explores this concept further, and I hope that in reading it ideas and thinking will be sparked off that will help other organizations promote their own culture of enquiry.

INTRODUCTION

Lesley Day

Over the last twenty years, there has been a profound shift in the philosophy and practices that underpin welfare services. We have seen the introduction of market principles into the provision of these services, and a split between "purchasers" and "providers" of welfare. In the NHS, there has been the introduction of the internal market—now being revised but not abandoned by the current Labour Government—and the emergence of ideas such as clinical governance, clinical audit, and evidenced-based practice, all designed to improve the standards of care and treatment for those with mental health problems.

These policy strategies are being implemented to "drive up quality" in the mental health services, partly by monitoring and improving the practices and professional development of those who work in these services (Dept. of Health, 1999). However, these policies and their implementation can be experienced by staff as dictats, particularly at a time when morale is low in the mental health system, beset by requirements to provide care in the community for the mentally ill and different forms of containment and residential care for those patients thought to be at risk of harming themselves or others.

This monograph is also focused on the need for enquiry into therapeutic practice, but it draws upon a different tradition, that of Tom Main's concepts of a "culture of enquiry" (1983) and "freedom from thought" (1967). In the latter paper, "Knowledge, Learning and Freedom from Thought", which is reproduced here in chapter one, Main argues that in both the individual and the institution, ideas and working practices introduced to ameliorate or attend to specific problems in the organization can become ritualized and repeated without real thought, and thus no longer serve as useful or creative responses to the primary task of the organization and the needs of the patients and staff. In other words, they move from the thinking space of the ego to the dictates of the superego. The dilemma is that while the "new" policies of clinical audit and governance can provide opportunities to enquire reflectively into our mental health systems and practices, they can easily become routinized procedures and bureaucratic practices, an institutional defence against creative thought and change. They may also feel imposed from the outside and be experienced as persecutory rather than as helpful to creative thought.

In thinking about staff and patients as a whole community, Main emphasized that for the hospital to be therapeutic, we need a "total culture of enquiry" if we are to "regularly examine, understand and perhaps resolve the tensions and defensive use of roles . . ." (1983, p. 136). We can become fixed on the idea of efficiency and changing structures but fail to recognize that it is the manner in which staff and patients relate to each other in these structures, the culture, that is vital to enquiry into the conscious and unconscious processes of the therapeutic organization.

As a therapeutic community, the "culture of enquiry" is central to the functioning of the Cassel Hospital, and in this monograph we illustrate this process by reflecting on different aspects of the inpatient treatment, inter-staff relations, and patient–staff relations. This exploration also highlights how we can be seduced into ritualized and non-thinking practices that affect the work with patients and staff relations. In his comment on Tom Main's paper, David Bell gives an example of his own experience, as a new consultant on the Adult Unit at the Cassel, of how an idea can become "hierarchically promoted". An interesting and important idea of Main's is that internal splits in the patient can manifest themselves in staff relationships, with different staff becoming identified with different aspects of the patient (Main, 1957). What Bell observed, from the fresh perspective of a new member of staff, was that this idea had been carved in stone and turned into a dogma—that if there were no splits in the staff group, then no real therapeutic work was occurring.

The contemporary Cassel Hospital was developed by Tom Main from 1946 to 1976 to create an institution that was self-exploratory of all of its systems, and this ethos continues into the present. Adults, adolescents, and families come into inpatient treatment often in a state of severe emotional and social breakdown. Different forms of abuse, deprivation, and traumatic loss are likely to have been a feature of their lives. Most of the patients have a history of more conventional psychiatric treatment as either outpatients or inpatients, with depression, psychotic breakdown, self-harm, and attempted suicide featuring in their backgrounds. The treatment programme of individual psychoanalytic psychotherapy, psychosocial nursing, and patients working actively with each other in the therapeutic community are described in this monograph, but with the specific aim of enquiring into some of these different practices and their successes, limitations, and difficulties.

In chapter two, Peter Griffiths and Bob Hinshelwood outline the specific structures within the hospital which sustain a culture of enquiry, but they point out that providing these structures does not mean they will always be used or protected. While the hospital, as a therapeutic community, must engage in reflective enquiry in the same way as its patients, we know that this process is difficult to sustain. It is these "lapses from continual enquiry" that the authors turn their attention to, in a wish to enquire into a culture of enquiry. They describe a number of manoeuvres, mostly unconscious, that inhibit a culture of enquiry: the packed timetable, the projection of despair, last-minutism, tribalism, interprofessional rivalries, pseudomutualism. Centrally, they focus on how a psychoanalytically informed therapeutic community such as the Cassel Hospital can be drawn into thinking that only the emotional space between the pair is what primarily needs to be enquired into. In concentrating on the difficulties engendered by the use of psychoanalytic psychotherapy within a therapeutic community, Griffiths and Hinshelwood are not arguing for a change of treatment approach. However, they do identify how inappropriate use of psychoanalytic ideas can close off enquiry.

In chapter three, Wilhelm Skogstad takes up a different but related theme by exploring how inpatient psychoanalytic psychotherapy, while it attempts to improve a person's internal and external functioning, may run the risk of building a "refuge" in which little or no real therapeutic work with the patient occurs. He demonstrates how the interrelated aspects of the treatment programme at the Cassel—the psychosocial nursing, the structures of the therapeutic community, and individual psychoanalytic psychotherapy—can be enquired into in order better to understand the interplay between the internal and external reality of the patient. Drawing upon four clinical examples, he identifies how a patient's difficulties and transference dynamics may simultaneously be worked with interpretatively in the psychotherapy and more practically in the living environment of the therapeutic community. This focus on external reality as well as internal reality also helps to act against the powerful regressive pull that patients can experience when in hospital.

In these clinical examples, Skogstad identifies the different layers of therapeutic work that go on in the hospital, and the method by which we need continually to enquire into them. The mutual interdependence of patients and staff is complex, as is the dynamics between them. Thus, we need continually to reflect upon the nature of the problem and where its origin may lie. While the therapeutic couple is one source for enquiry, Skogstad reaffirms that the organizational dynamics of the whole hospital need to be thought about.

In chapter four, Agata Pisula draws upon a theory of the psychology of social systems which integrates psychoanalytic and systems thinking as a way to reflect on how one structure within the hospital, the parents' meeting, was used to facilitate or hinder enquiry. The primary task of the parents' meeting, as defined by staff, is to provide a reflective space for parents in the Families Unit of the hospital to think about issues concerned with their children.

One aspect of this group that Pisula considers is the conscious and unconscious roles taken up by the facilitator and by herself as a nurse in the group. Pisula explores how the dynamics between the staff members within the group were reflected in the wider dynamics of the hospital at the time, thus pointing to the need to enquire into other parts of the system. This follows Main's contention that "we need to distinguish those disturbances that arise from inside a system from those that are merely reactive to the strains created by other related systems" (1983, p. 125). In identifying the unspoken issues and tensions in staff relations, and her own part in failing to enquire openly into these, she suggests that a useful therapeutic tool may have been lost.

Finally, in the chapter on the supervisory relationship, Pamela Pringle also explores the importance of reflecting on interstaff relations as part of a culture of enquiry, and the value of this in relation to the quality of the therapeutic work with patients. Here, the concern is the relationship between herself as a senior nurse with managerial responsibility for a nursing colleague. Pringle discusses the tensions in providing a containing space for this nurse in her own new role as a line manager.

Pringle analyses the difficulties in this supervisory relationship by drawing upon ideas about the different functions of supervision and the inherent tensions between them, as well as thinking about the ways in which patients can be drawn unconsciously into the conflicts in staff relationships, with latent characteristics of the staff offering a hook for projected aspects of the patient. Resolving the conscious and unconscious conflicts between staff was an important part of the treatment for the patient, as well as for the working relationship between the nurses. In this, a third person became important. This enabled a different kind of thinking to take place, and a creative approach to be adopted that focused on the use of constructive activity as a way of identifying the underlying destructiveness of the member of staff. This was implemented in relation to the work of the supervisee, but in a way it mirrored the kind of psychosocial nursing work undertaken with patients. It also shifted the relationship into a space where the focus could return to supporting the clinical work of the supervised nurse and thus improve the care of the patient and nursing practice.

As part of an NHS Trust, the Cassel Hospital is also involved in the process of implementing clinical audit and governance. However, perhaps what this monograph illustrates is that for a therapeutic community like the Cassel, enquiring into therapeutic practice is embedded in the culture of the institution and is not something new. Whether these "old" and "new" forms of enquiry can be complementary rather than in conflict is, of course, open to enquiry.

REFLECTIVE ENQUIRY
INTO
THERAPEUTIC INSTITUTIONS

CHAPTER ONE

Knowledge, learning, and freedom from thought

Tom Main

This chapter discusses the acquisition of knowledge by one generation from another, and the problems inherent in the process. The difficulties are seen as falling into three areas: (i) the difficulty of understanding the knowledge itself; (ii) the difficulty that a fact or a theory becomes an internal object subject to all the vicissitudes of object relations; and (iii) the difficulty of finding a training method that will enable the learner to assimilate knowledge and use it judiciously rather than to swallow it an uncomprehending way. Examples are drawn from the history of ideas in general, and from the author's experience of therapeutic communities, particularly the Cassel Hospital. The danger of allowing a body of knowledge to become, in its passage from one person to another, a mere set of never-to-be-questioned beliefs is illustrated. The common frailties of both trainers and trainees are discussed and methods suggested for understanding and overcoming them.

Abridged and reproduced by permission from *The Australian and New Zealand Journal of Psychiatry*, 1, 1967: 64–71.

The developments of knowledge, concepts, theories, and techniques represents man's attempts at mental mastery of his environment by ego processes. Ego mastery gives a certain kind of pleasure which comes, in part, from the replacement of feelings of helplessness in the face of a mysterious reality by feelings of *power* over it and competence at dealing with it; in part, also from narcissistic admiration at the *achievements* of the ego, through the successful exercise of its skills and strengths. The new knowledge itself is valued not only because it gives the ego a tool for dealing with immediate reality, but also because it gives *hope*— promise of future usefulness as an aid for mastering later situations.

But new knowledge, concepts, facts, and skills can also give pain, for they sometimes demand the abandoning or modification of old beliefs and practices that have been long cherished as familiar possessions, and now the enforced loss of favourite ideas and techniques will give rise to the protest, rage, and despair of mourning processes and to sad or resentful, nostalgic wishes for the good old days and the good old ideas.

It is well known in the history of science that the more it upsets an old-established order the more hotly new knowledge is resisted, but however true this may be as a generalization, we know that individuals vary much in their receptiveness to new ideas and in their loyalty to old ones. This is certainly a matter of individual character (which we can examine later), but the characteristic often varies with age. Notoriously, the young are eager to welcome the latest, one may say the youngest, ideas, partly because they are identified with them, whereas the old, who have much more to lose, are in general more loyal to old ideas. Moreover, whole cultures can vary in receptiveness and loyalty to ideas. Western society in the Middle Ages was characterized by stable adherence to the established order of things, by worship and dutiful repetition of what was known, by anger at dissidence, by punishment of heretics, and by the regular proscription of scepticism, free thought, and new knowledge. By contrast, in the last half-century, new knowledge rather than old has been eagerly valued. In a number of young revolutionary countries (such as the United States), ideas and techniques, if old, have been in general little worshipped, merely taken for granted; but, if new, have been delighted in, rapidly circulated, and eagerly used in the further mastery of the material world. For many people in such cultures, if a finding is modern it is also, apart from its usefulness, somehow a triumph, a victory not only over ignorance and helplessness but over the older order, as if this were mere ancestral dominance.

The reception of new knowledge thus often involves loving or aggressive impulses, feelings as well as the intellect. The complications so created seem to influence the uses to which knowledge is put, the fashions in knowledge, and all learning processes; however, before inquiring into them we must note the existence of mental energy that is neither loving nor aggressive, but, by fusion of these two extremes, is neutralized. An idea charged with neutralized mental energy will give no offence to, nor triumph over, existing understandings and will be greeted by sincere, sober thoughtfulness simply because it solves existing areas of shared puzzlement and offers the general pleasure of increased ego-mastery. We remember, however, that under states of frustration neutralized energy may defuse and revert to its original aggressive and loving components, or, in clinical terms, that sober assessment of fact tends under frustration to deteriorate into passions of love and hatred, that viewpoints and objectivity are then liable to be at their mercy, that new knowledge may become the stuff of politics and factions, and that the truths of an age may merely be its crushing majority vote.

Ideas indeed are psychological objects and are responded to—as are all psychological objects—by the whole mind. Perception is never a mentally isolated act, and it seems pointless to conduct experiments as if it were; for whatever else may happen to the perceived object, its mental fate will be much decided by the feelings it will always arouse—curiosity, distaste, guilt, liking, etc. A new idea may be recognized by the intellect as unmistakably to be reckoned with, but thereafter it is liable to suffer the same fate as any other—and to be used for emotional purposes.

This is the occasion not for a dissertation on object relations but for a mere reminder of how they concern the transmuting of body modes of primary experience into mental modes of experience.

Any object may be scotomized—or have a blind eye turned to it—because of the subject's preoccupation with other matters; or, because its existence is frightening, it can be mentally denied, so to speak, with tight-shut eyes. If the object is forcibly fed into the mind, it may be internalized in a particular oral way, mentally swallowed whole, thereafter to lie as an unassimilated foreign body, disturbing and preoccupying the mind, later perhaps to be mentally vomited, evacuated, or digested with more or less pain. The starved learner in particular may swallow an idea with eager undiscriminating delight and thereafter be preoccupied with it, in windy indigestion, to the exclusion of all other interest. Mental food may be used to create idle mental fat, or great energy and activity, or to whet the appetite for more. Pre-digested mental goods given in steady, dosed amounts may create a contented, well-fed, and placid taker, whereas the appetitive learner, who will not wait idly, but who quests for knowledge, seeks variety, and uses initiative and originality in the getting, seems to be created by more adventurous diets. New knowledge may be chewed over appreciatively or suspiciously for its nourishing or dangerous implications, or it may, with nihilism and contempt, have its usefulness destroyed, denigrated, or belittled, so that it quickly becomes a load of faeces—to use a neutral Latin word.

But there are more than intestinal modes of relating to objects. An idea may become a useful servant or a dominating master to be served devotedly and humbly for ever, a neglected orphan to be protected from others' criticism, an ideal to fight and die for, a tyrant to be placated with insincere lip-service or to be fought all one's life. It may be a friend, an ally against enemies, or a persecutor to be hated, a precise tool to be used along with others, proudly and skilfully, or it may become a ball-and-chain to be dragged into all situations. The possibilities are endless—because the possibilities of man's relations to his psychological objects, with various degrees and conformations of love and hatred, and various patterns of body-ego modes, are themselves endless. But they are also inevitable—and this is why the whole gamut of the feeling of which man is capable, from curiosity to loathing, from evangelism to competitiveness, always greets or becomes attached to ideas, areas of knowledge, theories, practices, and new facts. The conflict-free areas of the ego and their supplies of neutral energies are none too numerous, and although in any encounter with new ideas we can rely on some use of the reality-testing and synthetic functions of the ego, we can always reckon also on the ego as a whole remaining under its usual duress: from the unceasing operation of unconscious primitive moralities and the search for primitive satisfactions. We can expect the ego always to be in danger of seduction by the pleasure principle, away from the reality principle, and we can be sure that knowledge will always be in danger of being put to perverse use, in the services now of the id and now of the superego.

The fate of knowledge inside the mental apparatus is thus not at all ensured by its truthfulness or its usefulness in reality. An assiduous teaching of theories and facts, an honest sharing of discoveries, and a liberal training in skills give no guarantee that any will be learned and used appropriately. Even when they are well learned, there can be no certainty that the student will understand them in the manner intended by the trainer, still less that he or she will use them in the service of further thought. We can never be sure whether knowledge will form the basis of later initiative in thinking, learning, and the growth of techniques, or whether thorough training, far from equipping the individual for independent work, will only increase dependence on the trainer and his or her appetite for further passive experience, and thus inhibit his or her own thinking. Teaching can thus lead to an enrichment by knowledge or a crippling of the thinking capacity, and the phrase "well taught" can have sinister as well as satisfactory overtones. The trainer's hell is, of course, always paved with good intentions!

Difficulties in the learning process seem to lie in three areas. The difficulty of understanding the knowledge itself (because it may require considerable intellectual effort by the ego) is the first and the one most recognized by almost everybody. The difficulty that a fact or a theory becomes an internal object, subject to all the vicissitudes of object relations and of defused energies, is the second and is rarely studied by anybody except psychoanalysts. The third difficulty is that of training methods, which are well studied only by educationists. The communications we offer to our patients, to our colleagues in our writings and lectures, to our juniors in their training, and to our staffs in institutions may all fail to have the effects we intended because of one or other of these three types of difficulties. I now confine myself to some aspects of the third difficulty, that of the training method, which of course includes the trainer–trainee relationship, and I will discuss in some detail a single socio-clinical example.

The promotion of an idea

At the Cassel Hospital, groups of nurses, doctors, and neurotic patients met over a long period to examine the existing roles of patients and staff, and their relevance for therapy. It soon emerged that many hospital roles and their emergent procedures had little relevance to, and some seemed actually to be at variance with, our declared aims: of freeing the ego from unconscious enslavement and promoting mental integration.

These discussions were strainful but enjoyable. Our findings were many and led us to new minor theories upon which we decided to base various experiments with hospital techniques and procedures. Like all theories, ours were tentative, and as we could not be certain of the outcome of our experiments we were prepared to abandon or alter any new procedures that did not work well. For my present purpose, I will select one simple emergent procedure: patients should be enabled to go home for the weekend if they so wish. This stemmed from our clinical findings that some patients became acculturated for hospital life only, unfitted for any other. It had become clear that by arranging severance of patients' important relationships with home and work we had been blindly colluding with, rather than tolerantly examining, our patients' wishes for social regression. Making hospital life an all-or-none matter had prevented us and them from learning anything about the anxieties or resentments that underlay their acceptance of the abnormal way of life of seven-days-a-week hospitalization. We were aware that such a regression was important for some and perhaps should be catered for, but we had to recognize that our hospital system was unthinkingly imposing, upon all, automatic childlike roles of obedient passivity or rebellious invalidism at the expense of initiative and responsibleness. Now we sought to create conditions where patients could use the hospital for as many or as few nights a week as they wished, and staff could become students of this behaviour rather than controllers of it.

We therefore made it easy for patients to go home for the week-end (as well as on other days). They simply decided for themselves, made their own arrangements, and asked no permission of any-body, but as in any household told the patient's catering committee what meals they would be away for and when they thought they would be back. Those who did not wish to go home were free to stay in hospital.

I do not wish to discuss whether all this was wise or unwise, but only to emphasize that it was a new idea for us. It required all of us to give up our older safe procedures, but we did so (with more or less resistance) because it promised in its own small way to make more sense of our work, in that it would allow behaviour to be based more on ego choices of patients and less on staff-based disci-plines.

For some years thereafter, all went smoothly and unremark-ably. We were able to recognize more the problems of those who in hospital hid from life. We continued to cater for massive regres-sion, but we no longer imposed invalidism on all. Many patients never lost adult contact with their homes and work places; dehabil-itation was avoided, and rehabilitation was less of a problem on discharge.

We were satisfied with our small experiment, and when new staff joined us they too joined in the thinking and helped to make the idea work. In turn, as the years passed, they showed later generations of staff how things were and would speak happily, even proudly, about the theory and the practice.

Several years later, most of the patients were still going home at weekends, but now it had become the thing to do, and a kind of moralism had crept into the procedures. Patients who were too distressed to go home had somehow become cultural oddities, and the climate around them was vaguely disapproving. Fewer nurses were needed at weekends now, and weekend duty for nurses had become a nuisance. There were subtle but recognizable pressures on all patients to go home at weekends. Something was not quite right.

The officialese of the hospital was still about patients being free to choose about their weekends, but these words were now mere relics of an idea and no longer representative of a living truth. What had originally been a useful idea and a break from thoughtless discipline was itself becoming a new kind of thoughtless discipline.

My awareness of all this is the result only of hindsight, for I woke up to the situation late, and only after hearing a careless remark of a fairly new nurse. In casual conversation, she talked of a difficult patient whom she had tried to *persuade* to go home. When asked about this, she said confidently that it would be *good* for the patient and later that it was *good* for *all* patients to go home. It became clear that her patients were quite free to choose only what she wanted. This nurse's pronouncement was not typical of all our nurses, but, for her at least, a blanket prejudgment was being used where a readiness to think out the uniqueness of each case had been aimed at. A fixed procedure had emerged out of a flexible technique, and an idea had become a morality. What had begun as a free ego-choice had grown into a fixed discipline. It was no longer that a particular choice could be relevant, characteristic, singular, useful, or interesting; it had become either *good* or *bad*, a matter for conformance and not thought, an affair of the nurse's superego and not her ego.

This one example shows how an idea, passed from one person to another by teaching, can change its mental residence, moving from the experimental and thinking areas of the ego of one generation into the fixed-morality areas, the ego-ideal and the superego, of the next. I will call this the *hierarchical promotion* of ideas between the generations, and I must interrupt my clinical example to draw attention to its social importance and frequency.

Hierarchical promotion is a fate that threatens all knowledge. From their early regard as interesting mental tools to be taken up or discarded skilfully according to their usefulness for the task in hand, ideas are liable to become, in their passage from one person to another, mere *beliefs*, sets of never-to-be-questioned, always to-be-believed rules, which now handicap further thought.

The movement between the generations from the pleasure or neutral areas of the ego into the fixed-control areas is insidious and difficult to detect. It is tempting to leaders to be pleased with their acolytes for believing their ideas, and it is not a simple matter to suspect one's most ardent followers of having little capacity for thought or understanding. It is not at all easy to distinguish those who possess an idea from those who are possessed by it, to distinguish thought from belief, and yet, recognizably often, good disciples are merely compulsive practitioners of knowledge as a morality rather than thinkers and users of it.

The danger of becoming culture-bound, of being enmeshed unthinkingly in moral beliefs and beloved practices that were once reality-oriented ideas and techniques, is of course feared and fought in those organizations where efficiency over a task can be measured. In industries where profits measure social efficiency, industrial consultants are regularly called in to avert this danger, and some of their functions are similar to those of the psychotherapist. They set out to study the ways archaic modes of operating persist beyond their usefulness and not only bind up large amounts of energy in non-productive activities, but lead to blind rules of practice which hamper free thinking and creativity. I do not need to emphasize the storms of difficulty that arise in some instances when workers or management are asked to give up their old beloved ways in favour of new ones.

This difficulty, of transmitting knowledge from one generation to another as a set of tools for skilled use and skilled amendment rather than as sets of restricting disciplines, is not therefore peculiar to the refreshment of psychiatry. The clinging to the forms rather than to the purposes is a regular well-known human activity in all areas of knowledge. It accounts for the slow accretions of currently meaningless traditions and for the increase in decadent (i.e. non-functional) activities, which eventually overtake all societies and even whole civilizations. The danger for organized societies is that the knowledge and skill that go towards their creation may through the generations cease to be used for ego-mastery and instead be used for ego-restrictions through the practice or worshipped beliefs and procedures that were once ideas and techniques. In contrast to Freud's therapeutic hopes that where id was ego shall be, the danger of the process for all knowledge and for all training is that where ego was superego shall be.

But what influences *hierarchical promotion* between the generations? How does it happen? I return to my example in the hope that it can help. I shall, of course, ignore the contributions of medical staff to the events in question and concentrate on the nursing staff's difficulties. This is in the usual psychiatric hospital tradition, is easier, and hurts doctors less.

All the new nurses were postgraduates, from general or psychiatric hospitals. The training method was sophisticated and consisted of seminars whereat the tutor was not concerned to instil her own ideas but to help her students to think about and digest their daily clinical experiences.

The earliest generation of nurses, who, with doctors as equals, examined patient-and-staff roles and designed new powers, responsibilities, and procedures, had to think hard. In arriving at the idea of patients freely visiting their homes, they overcame within themselves and between each other all sorts of traditional resistances in argument and discussion. Thereafter, they undertook cautious experiments, for at that time there were no precedents. They were proud of their efforts, learned much, and owned the idea in well-digested form, and they used the practice as their own. They therefore gladly shared these in living form with the next generation of nurses, and three years later these too had thought things out (chewed things over), conducted experiments, and now also carried out thoughtful and skilful practice. But with successive generations of nurses, two things happened. First, the idea ceased to be new or unusual, and practice became confident and unremarkable. Second, the method of passing these on altered, in that the doubts and resistances of new nurses were treated with less patience and understanding. The reasons were ordinary enough.

More recent problems and technique had occupied the senior nurses' thinking and they no longer had the inclination to allow newcomers to discover the idea for themselves, or to chew it over in argument, to take time to digest it, to think how it could go wrong, to try it out and make errors for themselves, to discuss the results, and to value their own experiences; the whole thing was now working well, and all variations, additions, modifications, and new applications had been worked over. The older nurses saw no reason why a new one should hesitate. They were sure, and although their teaching was benevolent and generous it was no longer tentative. Perhaps they were now too far from their own early doubts and conflicts to be interested when these arose afresh in their students. They had done the thinking, and they wanted to save the newcomers from having to do it all again.

The newcomers thus had to accept (swallow) it obediently as the privileged neophytes of respected and kindly trainers. The idea was interesting, authoritative, and made good intellectual sense, but that was all. It did not offer them mastery of any immediate clinical problems, nor clarify pressing confusions—for they were experiencing neither. They thus acquired the idea in a way utterly different from that of the first generation of nurses, and they apparently installed it in a different mental area. The original nurses had hammered out the idea and the practice as co-equals sharing unsolved problems, but the co-equality of ignorance could not be offered the newcomers, for now there were only helpful experts and eager beginners in this matter. The appetitive, problem-solving, active learning of the first generation was in contrast with the merely obedient and passive learning of the last.

Such a system—of experts and beginners—is an inevitable development, with all knowledge a matter of our common reality. Neither knowledge nor expertise is to be denied, but by themselves they are not the cause of hierarchical promotion in newcomers. It is the *way* the expert uses his or her knowledge in training which much influences whether the knowledge will be used for the growth of ideas, skills, and new thinking: for the formation of ideals to follow, in hope or in despairing inferiority; for more scholarship and endless repetition; for ego-restrictions on further thought by the practice of knowledge as a binding religion—in short, whether the knowledge will be used for the enrichment of the ego, the ego-defences, the ego-ideal, or the superego.

I have to add that in my homely example our experts had also become seniors holding not only more knowledge but more power in the hospital. Now, to argue with an expert is one thing, a privilege all learners should have, but to argue with one's boss is another, a piece of career-folly, tactless at best, suicidal at worst. If the trainer also holds *power to promote* the student within a social hierarchy, chewing over the expert's ideas critically and thoughtfully is liable to be at a discount, a matter of badness, guilt, or danger, whereas swallowing the idea whole in glad or obedient conformance is liable to be at a premium, for it is the safe and even the right and good thing. With our newest nurses, the ideas offered were liable to be coloured not merely by usefulness but by power, rightness, and goodness, and therefore to burden the ego and enrich the superego.

My example can make room for the *difference between individuals* over how they may greet new knowledge. Firstly, the nurse who used her training as a morality was not typical of the nursing staff as a whole but had the kind of mind that tended to belief rather than thought. Secondly, at the time of my observation she was also not at her best, being in great frustration over a tragic matter in her private life. I mention these two points, firstly to draw attention to the way individuals vary in the way they use knowledge (as a working tool, as a model of proper thought, as a persecutor, as an ideal to be burdened with, etc.), and secondly to emphasize that under frustration the superego is frequently reinforced and then makes use of ideas that were hitherto the possession of the ego—in short, that *hierarchical promotion* occurs in states of frustration. (We all know how we may use our knowledge for purposes of reprimand when we are in a bad temper.) Lastly, we cannot avoid noticing that in not permitting the patient to think for himself the nurse was perhaps only *doing what she felt had been done* to her in her own training, and that she was dominated by an introject, "identified with the aggressor".

Training methods

All learners, of course, identify to some extent with their trainers. If we are to train at all, the most we can do is to understand the various kinds of identification and how they occur and then to devise a technique that can best produce the results we seek. Identification being a wide-ranging matter, trainees learn not merely from what their trainers teach or preach, but from what they practise, and not only from what they do, but what they imply; from what they love and what they hate; and what they do not do; and what they take for granted. If the trainer is less interested in imparting facts than in thinking and allowing his or her trainees to think for themselves, then the trainees too will grant to themselves, and later to others, the right to think about facts. Contrariwise, if the trainer is concerned not with thinking and choosing but only with knowledge and views then the trainees will be filled with knowledge and views that they may later repeat and enlarge—but they will not think much.

The form of the training is thus as important for the result as is the content. It is not the expertise or the knowledge itself that decide how far these will be used to enlarge the ego, the ego-ideal, or the superego, but (ignoring the variations between trainees) the manner of the trainer, his or her attitude, firstly to the knowledge itself (as a toy, a tool, a servant, an ideal, a master, a god, etc.) and secondly to the trainee him/herself (an inferior to be encouraged or bullied, an equal to be respected, agreed with, fought with, soothed, stimulated, a rival to be denigrated and subdued, etc.). It is the identification with these aspects of the trainer that decides so much.

Enthusiasm or popularity in a trainer is therefore no criterion of excellence. The popular trainer may be one who simply creates dependency. The enthusiastic installer of original findings may, as our example showed, be indeed a crusher of originality, or not—it depends on *how* the trainer uses his or her enthusiasms: whether for the free operation of zestful thinking or the installing of knowledge by the discouragement of independence, doubt, disagreement, experiment, or chewing over.

We can see that forceful, sure teaching by an authority seems to hasten the process whereby an idea degenerates into a belief by hierarchical promotion, and how the clear expositor who knows best is most likely to produce this result. Disciplinary and forceful sure teaching offers few choices to the student; he or she can reject all angrily while hypocritically pretending not to, or can swallow it and become a well-fed slave—an obedient but uninspired representative of the teacher's school, dutiful in using and expanding its ideas but afraid to move into fresh fields and think for him/herself. Some teachers produce only identifications with teachers, all in the chain conforming with and idealizing their teachers and using knowledge with compulsive serenity in the service of the super-teacher, eventually an aspect of the superego. The nurse in my example did this.

This process is not without importance for those concerned with the study of inanimate things in the pure sciences, and indeed some material scientists are already concerned about it. But where the subject of the work is another human being, as in the psychotherapy profession, it is of vital importance. For a human being—a patient—to be used merely as a recipient for correctly taught knowledge or advice of a doctor cannot help any problem that requires both doctor and patient to study and discover together and think about the unique features of the individual and his or her troubles. Thus the desirable identification-model offered by a *trainer* for future work with humans must itself somehow demonstrate readiness: to listen to each trainee's difficulties, to tolerate their existence and to help the trainee recognize and think about them for him/herself; to avoid riding over his or her difficulties with expert advice or knowledge but to require him or her to retain responsibility for solving his or her problems; to view hasty action, helplessness, or ignorance as defences against the pain of situations which need further enquiry and fuller understanding; to begin with ignorance and preparedness to study every problem anew and to think afresh about each trainee's ways of working; not to fall back when puzzled or frustrated on the views of learned authorities or on other ideal knowledge residing in or near the superego but to admit puzzlement and frustration when these arise. This model is of a worker who is not powerful in *scholarship* but in *skill* with human problems.

In short, we who work with human beings need a new method of training. The kind, keen trainer who freely offers knowledge as a solution to ignorance can only create grateful obedient dependency in his or her pupils and is not useful as a model of identification for future doctor–patient relations. The forceful teacher who disciplines his or her pupils and keeps them from idleness or ignorance will be no better for our future psychiatrists. Our professional model cannot be based on adding to ego-regression and enslavement by clever or superior knowledge, or with further oppression by further introjects into the superego. Just as we need skills to help our patients discover within themselves new strengths and independent capacities and to free them from old restrictions and dependence on archaic authorities, so we need a training method that can allow the trainer to demonstrate these very skills in a model training relationship. And just as we have to aim at our patients becoming adults co-equal with ourselves, so our training should seek to be based on human equality between trainer and trainee, and forgo authority and power and all status except that which emerges from expertness among co-equal workmen of enquiry. Just as we eschew telling our patients what to think or believe, the new model will eschew our telling our trainees.

We do not possess such a model. Perhaps we are still too tyrannized by what our own teachers did to us, too faithful in enslavement to them, to break new ground. But there are stirrings. Michael Balint (1957) has gone some way towards creating a method that is concerned not to teach but to train, that avoids the instilling of "correct" ideas or the solving by the trainer of the trainees' ignorance but is aimed at helping trainees find the courage to use their own resources to think their own way through their clinical problems, to study the effects of their own prejudices and interventions on their patients' illnesses, and to develop not static psychiatric knowledge but living psychiatric techniques.

Following Balint's lead, a number of others in different countries have made experiments with similar aims. They have one thing in common—they offer low dosages of training and extend over a long period to allow full time for digestion and the development of fresh hungers. They are not full-time intensive, indigestible crash courses of some days or weeks but are usually patterned once-weekly for some years. Scholarship is sparingly exhibited, and discussion is kept geared to the immediate clinical work of the trainers, but there are frequent demonstrations of the technical handling by the trainer of the difficulties that trainees may have in the immediate present, with their work, their fellow trainees, or the trainer. The trainees are not generously or force-fed, and not fed with general principles when they demand knowledge and rescue from immediate clinical puzzlement; rather, they are kept hungry, and questing, and are helped to use their own experiences to hammer out principles and to regard thinking as their proper contribution towards joint research. The aim is not to produce scholars, but skilled craftsmen who can work with human suffering; not to enlarge the authority areas of the ego, but the executive working areas.

This may sound ideal, but those of us who use this training method do not, in spite of awareness of the dangers, avoid results that show tyrannical introjections of the trainer, dependence on *his or her* ego rather than independence from it, idealization of some feature of his or hers, identification with some of his or her aspects, favourite phrases, methods of working, etc., usually in caricatured and distorted versions. In brief, although we are generally satisfied that this training method avoids the big pitfalls inherent in thoughtless adherence to traditional teaching, the results are far from perfect.

In some trainees, the results are not even worthwhile and are only the old extremes—either total rejection of the training, in the sense that despite increased knowledge the trainee is unchanged in capacity for independent thought and action; or a total identification, in that the trainee becomes a mere long-player (as did our nurse) of the trainer's ideas and skills, applying them as if possessed in *hierarchical promotion*. One or two have even sought psychoanalytic training, apparently only to further slavishly the demands of the newly introjected trainer in the superego for absolute conformance, on the old pattern of being taught to become only another teacher.

Now, although such results are common enough in traditional training methods, and relatively rare in this newer method, they have to be taken seriously. For the new method has been developed to avoid such results. How do they arise? Is it a fault in the method? In the trainer? Or in the trainee?

As used, the method contains faults. The trainers at the Cassel Hospital concerned in developing it meet regularly to discuss their training technique, and all—despite declared plans to the contrary—have occasionally strayed from the aim of seeking out and identifying the strains in the doctor–patient relationship and led (trainees) to sudden regression, non-thinking, and dependence on the trainer. All the times have yielded to trainees' requests for teaching and for the trainer to solve their problems. None has been able to avoid the occasional use of censure or disapproval (usually disguised as a neutral question or remark). None of us has always been able to note quickly enough and to bring to full-enough awareness baneful identifications with the trainer. The method is by no means easy and asks a lot of the trainers, so some failures are inevitable. But these seem to arise less out of the method than out of faults in the trainers' skills. Are the faults then in the trainers?

Here I can speak for myself and must confess that I am some-times a hierarchical promoter of ideas, despite good intentions to the contrary. I find it difficult at times not to use ideas, which were once ego possessions, forcefully in the service of the superego. But again this seems to me to have some inevitability; *hierarchical pro-motion* is not only an intergenerational process but an intrapsychic one within the *individual*.

To begin with, a new idea is a more or less hardly won tool for use among equals, with no authority other than that. Its winning may give pleasure or pride, and the idea itself may give pleasure (because of its powers of mastery of a problem), and after further reality-testing by the ego it can also become *trusted*. It now has some authority of its own and is accorded an appropriate place in the hierarchical network of ideas in the ego of the individual con-cerned. Once the idea is installed in the hierarchy, the ego-work that gave rise to the idea often becomes, however, slowly de-cathected. The affective pains and excitement of the discovery and the mode of the idea's internalization may become valued and remembered less than the idea itself. (People vary considerably in this matter, and here Balint's ideas of ocnophilic and philobatic characters are relevant.) Now the idea alone, objectified and stripped of its subjective connections, may be installed in the preconscious memory systems of the ego, whence it can be re-cathected by neutral energies and recalled as occasion requires. The idea will now be accepted rather than thought about, having achieved a firmly sheltered and stored life of its own in the system of interlinked ideas. This secondary situation can be more or less conflict-free, concerned only with neutral energies and values.

But the usual assumption that recall uses mostly neutral energy ignores the frequency and inevitability of energy-defusion (after frustration especially) and man's tendency to love and idealize his possessions. An idea often becomes invested with non-neutral energy, thereafter becoming animistically a household god, for instance, or a part of the narcissitically valued self; with the pas-sage of time, a trusted familiar, perhaps even a valued protected favourite. *Depending on the way it was obtained, tested, and installed,* an idea may thus be charged with pride, idealizing love, certainty, or hatred and malice, and so forth. To doubt it now or to examine it afresh is not merely economically wasteful (in view of all the earlier mental work of reality-testing and the ego-synthesis and energy-distribution of the past) but emotionally painful; and any such attempts may (varying with the person) be resisted by the ego as narcissistically wounding, threatening its former achievements, reliability, and security or its beloved possessions.

Thus an idea can change its residence from the initial plastic area of the ego, where it may be linked with various affects of triumph and mastery, to an objective neutral area and, later still, to an area of sureness in which it becomes beyond review, criticism, or contention. It may now become a captor of the self and the thinking processes. It may be submitted to as an authority, or loved as an old comrade-in-arms, or treasured as a precious anchorage, to be defended for ever from internal or external attack by thought-ful review. Its use in thinking processes is now that of a given truth, to be turned to in trouble or doubt for comfort when all else fails. The growth of attitudes of doubt-free belief, loyalty, treasuring, defending, and relying are of course those concerned with idealiz-ing love and clinging identification and (to use my term) with *hierarchical promotion*: away from living thought towards static be-lief, away from technique towards procedure, away from an idea towards a morality, and away from the pleasure-ego of enjoyment and the neutral-ego of objectivity towards the worshipful areas of the ego-ideal and the tyrannical absolutes of the superego.

Trainers themselves are not exempt from this process of hierar-chical promotion. Each generation acquires new knowledge by pain and effort and then seeks to hand on to the next generation this new knowledge in the vain hope of saving it the pain of discov-ery. Fathers do this with their sons, mothers with their daughters; eagerly, imploringly, and even desperately they ask them to accept the findings as an idealized gift. But, however sad, there is no short-cut to knowledge for the young. They have to learn for them-selves and cannot usefully be saved from strains, from errors, and from time-wasting finding out for themselves if they are to become able, rather then well-fed, people. They cannot without penalty to their future as thinkers give a high place in their own hierarchy of thought to the treasured and impelled ideas of their elders merely because their elders forcibly want them to. The learner's right to

think for him/herself is thus often at odds with the trainer's eagerness that the learner should accept the tested and useful beliefs and
standards of another. Cooperative obedience and non-thinking
conformity and loving superego-coloured behaviour in the young
is one danger with intergenerational *hierarchical promotion*. The
other is that anger of the old at the ingratitude of the young will
lead to helpless introjection and idealization on the one hand or
rejection and denigration on the other. A sad recognition of this
dilemma occurs in the French saying, "*Si jeunesse savait, si vieillesse
pouvait*".

I have my own favourite ideas, and I must confess that in
moments of frustration (when I did not suffer fools gladly or did
not understand a difficulty in the discussion with my trainees) I
have punched these home purely as authoritative givens. I have
not always offered them only as possibilities that might—or might
not—be of use of interest to the trainee about the case under discussion, and I know that my fellow trainers have similar failings,
despite all our decisions to avoid forceful pluggings of our own
ideas. Our trainees have all been exposed to our failing, but only
certain trainees have done poorly. Our gross mistakes are not too
frequent, we have some skill, we try to be alert to various trainees'
difficulties, and we meet with some success. How far, then, are our
failures due to faults in the trainees?

In general, our trainees have the same frailties as all human
beings in training. The pitfalls they lay for the trainer are the usual
ones: a readiness to listen to the trainer; an eagerness to split off
criticism, to idealize and identify with the trainer, a turning to the
trainer for rescue when in trouble; respect for the trainer as someone akin to Santa Claus, who will bring regressively free unearned
gifts.* These general pitfalls always include the readiness of learners to offer respect before it is earned; to be obedient, dependent,
insatiable, childlike; to regress into credulous absorptive states and
to accept all; to hide and deny all rebelliousness, anger, and adult
capacities for reflective critical thought; and to project all their wits
and adulthood into the trainer (just as some patients do). The

---

*Like the Devil, Santa Claus is the child's father.

training technique used for avoiding these pitfalls (and for dealing with their opposites—compulsive argument and rejection of all knowledge) have been the same as for clinical work—namely, to identify these primitive elements in the unconsciously sought and offered relationship, to avoid collusive response to them, to refuse to behave in ways that foster these attitudes, but to concentrate on and lay bare the nature of the immediate anxieties. This does *not* mean that training must become therapy: only that the trainer and trainee together identify the strains that the patient creates in the doctor and which then threaten the doctor's capacity for cool observation and thought and lead him or her to regressive forms of doctoring (preaching, cleverness, blindness, refuge in authority, etc.)

The handling of these general features of trainee groups is routine (but not easy) work in the training technique I have mentioned. The rewards for the trainer who has managed them reasonably well has been a trainee who is fairly skilled and independently thoughtful in his work, able to stand the strains of not knowing, able at using his or her knowledge selectively and thoughtfully rather than dutifully and compulsively, not as a set of fixed responses and generalized procedures for all patients, but as the basis for devising fresh responses appropriate for each patient situation as it develops.

But if the technique is fairly good and the pitfalls fairly well recognized, if the trainers discern and handle the problems with fair sensitivity and care, how then to explain the worst failures— massive insensitivity to or total identification with the training?

I have noticed that my own failures occurred in those whose former learning had also been dealt with, sometimes from childhood, by hierarchical promotion into fixed idealized systems. Any further training that required modification of their former ideas therefore aroused in these trainees an indignant moral defence of their older idea-beliefs. These seemed to tyrannize them, so that they took little interest in other ideas and, indeed, could not tolerate any that ran counter to their fixed-idea systems. It was as if their knowledge was not fluid but solid, and that their ideas were used not as a springboard for new adventures in thought, but for safety and, indeed, for mental protection *against* the adventure of thinking. They sought of their training not new problems to solve but more opportunities to exercise what they already knew, or new authority for facts to believe in, to which they might cling for safety in future work crises. The need of these trainees was to be told by another; anxious when faced with fresh situations, they turned to authority or authority-given ideas to save them. They mistrusted the value of thinking for themselves, and some would openly declare it to be dangerous for their patients. In their need to find safety from thought, a few had become widely read, one or two even scholarly, ready to quote authorities when in trouble with new problems. They sought to seduce the trainer to become yet another authority, and, as I have reported, this trainer sometimes fell for it.

Some people thus have a tendency to value knowledge for its authority rather than for usefulness in thinking, and it is difficult, perhaps impossible, to create a training that will enable them to use ideas rather than be used by them. Certain trainees seek in knowledge a system of law-giving, a guide about what they are allowed to think. Knowledge, concepts, theories, and techniques are installed in the morality areas of the mind rather as regulating parents and not as co-equal friends available for ego-work. They can easily be taught, but they cannot at present be trained.

I do not know what the percentage of such people is in any trainee population, but I suspect that it is high in any group that clings dutifully to authoritative organizations for higher learning rather than seeks early independence and private adventure. In any event, the *hierarchical promotion* of ideas is a process common to all mankind, and how far and how fast any individual carries it out is a question only of degree. As I have tried to indicate, the use of knowledge as a defence against thought can be a matter of character; secondly, it is a common product of certain prolonged training methods; and thirdly, it is a product of certain forceful trainers. It is likely that these trainers themselves prefer knowledge to thought, because it gives safety against uncertainty, and, through *hierarchical promotion*, they worship knowledge not so much for its usefulness as for an end in itself. One must acknowledge that economic temptation by the superego regularly allows it to conquer areas of the ego. The superego offers short-cuts and saves us from the strains of thinking, for it always in reality lets us know what to do and what not to do. The ego need not choose now and is saved work.

Lastly, hierarchical promotion takes time, and seems to be a cumulative process. The elderly, who have no living parents as their authorities, perhaps use it most. Notoriously they often draw their safety from old ideas, which have been hierarchically promoted and which they cannot give up. The increasing mental rigidity of age may therefore owe something to the mental process I have described.

Comment

David Bell

About a week before he died, I wrote to Tom Main, letting him know how important this paper, "Knowledge, Learning, and Freedom from Thought", had been for me. I am pleased to be involved in its publication here so that it can reach a wider readership. Apparently it was written on an aeroplane during an attack of dysentery, and Main thought it not well written—a view I do not share! I first came across the paper shortly after my arrival at the Cassel, when it was presented at a journal club by a senior registrar (Toby Thompson, to whom I remain indebted). Since then I have found myself referring to it in various different contexts. It is a paper of relevance not only to work in institutions but to psychoanalysis in general. It also raises some very important issues concerning the training of psychoanalysts, which I return to later.

Anyone who has worked in an institution is especially sensitized to the issues raised by this paper. The degradation of ideas into meaningless ritual is a phenomenon especially visible in groups and institutions. I find much in common between the ideas expressed in this paper and certain of Bion's ideas—initially also formulated in his papers on groups. As is well known, both Main and Bion were involved in the famous Northfield experiment—a flowering of interest in groups and institutional processes just after the Second World War.

There is, I believe, an important continuity between Bion's work on groups and his later papers on psychotic processes. It was the group work that led to his interest in those processes in a group which act against thinking and the pursuit of knowledge. Bion later developed these ideas in his papers on psychoses. Main applied the ideas he developed during this period to the therapeutic and anti-

Abridged and reproduced by permission from *Psychoanalytic Psychotherapy*, 5 (1), 1990: 74–78.

therapeutic aspects of institutions. He makes clear in this paper the wider relevance of these ideas.

Firstly, I would like briefly to discuss the relevance of this paper to the work at the Cassel. Main has said elsewhere that the term "therapeutic community" does not define any particular technique or procedure but, rather, a particular form of social organization which creates a "culture of enquiry". Main stresses in this paper the vital importance of battling against those processes that transform thought-provoking ideas into dogmas to be worshipped. I can think of numerous examples that are of a very similar nature to the example in the paper.

For instance, it is a very interesting notion that patients in an institution often have the capacity to create situations in which various members of staff come to contain and become identified with different aspects of the patient. This leads to a situation in which internal splits, often of a psychotic intensity, become manifest in the relationships between various staff members who have become identified with different aspects of the patient. Main described this very elegantly in his paper "The Ailment" (1957). This understanding led to methods of dealing with such situations—for example, creating a context in which the disturbances between staff can be understood as having important communicative value that can be used to further the understanding of the patient.

However, this interesting and thought-provoking idea had become something quite different when I arrived on the Adult Unit at the Cassel, to which I had been appointed. As Main demonstrates in the paper, the idea had "moved its residence" and been "hierarchically promoted". Staff stated that *all* patients cause splits between staff, and the *only* way to help patients was to "confront" them—which sometimes meant attempting to prevent any splitting. Often I found that a nurse and psychotherapist were sharing rather similar difficulties in their relationship with a particular patient, expressed differently in the different contexts. However, an atmosphere had been created in which it was almost impossible to have this thought—perhaps only a newcomer could have it. There was a dominant view that dictated that if there was no "split" between staff being addressed, then no therapeutic work was taking place. The word "splitting", then, had become fetishized and lost its meaning. Along with this fetishization there was a concretization, as though the real splits were not in the patient's mind but in the disputes between staff members and could only be remedied by meetings between patient and the members of staff involved. There were certain circumstances that had led to this situation. Most importantly, the unit had not had a permanent consultant for a long period of time. There were considerably anxieties about authority, and the senior nurse, who was bearing much of the strain, had been relatively unsupported. Driven by anxiety, she had developed a form of practice that had generated a defensive social system that prohibited thought and doubt, these processes having been replaced by procedures and rituals. This situation, because it was so extreme, was easy to see, but these forces can also act in a very subtle way and, at least in my experience, are ever-present.

The replacement of thought by these ritualized practices acts as a defence against very primitive dreads of "not-knowing". The pursuit of knowledge, which contains thought and doubt, is replaced by the demand for omnipotence, an omnipotence that can become very tyrannical. An example of this transformation can often be found in the procedure, so common in all hospitals, called "feeding back". An understandable wish to encourage the free flow of information concerning patients as and when necessary turns into a demand for endless meetings where information is fed back from other meetings. The feedback process swells up until there is no room for discussion or thought. This process, though initiated by the anxiety of "not-knowing", becomes driven by a dread of being blamed for some untoward circumstance—such as suicide. Again, as Main describes in this paper, an ego function—handing on of information—has been replaced by a superego function. The character of this superego bears a great resemblance to that found in psychotic patients, as described by Rosenfeld (1965).* It is, of course, sometimes much easier to investigate these processes in patients rather than in staff. I can think of patient

---

*I am reminded of a psychotic patient who would spend his weekly session "filling me in" with what had happened since the last session—a list of facts stripped of any thought-provoking function. This activity was necessary to placate a terrifying superego (projected into me), which had to be told everything. It generated a hatred of doubt—and therefore of thought.

groups where, for example, the idea that it might be useful to become acquainted with certain thoughts or states of mind that have been hitherto resisted is transformed into a ritual called "talking about feelings". It is as if there is a shared belief that the god (doctors or nurses) will grant relief from suffering if the patients express their feelings. If one patient actually experiences genuine affect, he or she may be very envied, or be hailed for his or her achievement—cure is expected soon. Again, an idea has degenerated into the dogma of a religious cult. Psychoanalysts who work in institutions are very familiar with this degeneration of psychoanalytic thinking.

To turn for a moment to psychoanalytic practice, the phenomenon that Main is describing is, I think, very often found in the consulting-room. The patient picks up various of the analyst's ideas (again, as Bion has described, he becomes an expert on the analyst's theories) but subtly transforms them. I have a patient who learnt that if he violently turned away from me during a break, and so destroyed me in his mind as a helpful object, he became ill during the break. He found this understanding helpful, and it led to some progress in the analytic work. This understanding, however, soon turned into something quite different. In one session, before a break, he described feeling better: he had enjoyed his work. (This was a major achievement for him as he had always found work so persecuting. It represented an unconscious identification with the helpful analytic work.) Suddenly, on his way to his session he became gripped by a terror that resulted from the fact that he had not been consciously thinking about me or the coming break. He then forced himself to think about me and the coming break, as he believed that if he did not he would become ill. Again, here I think one can see how understanding is taken over by a tyrannical omnipotence and transformed into a procedure, in just the way Main described in this paper.

I would now like to turn briefly to the issues raised in this paper in regard to training. Main raises a particularly interesting problem—namely, how do ideas and experiences, won through hard work, get handed on to the next generation? Main emphasizes how a "hierarchical promotion" of ideas often takes place at this point, and I think that this is a central problem for psychoanalytic training. Obviously the most important features will be in helping a candidate think for him/herself. Supervision has not only positive effects but also negative effects that are easily missed. I think trainees often make very powerful identifications with supervisors—identifications that actually act against learning. Although a supervisor may think that he or she is helping a trainee to think about the material, quite often something occurs that is more akin to the enactments that I have referred to in patients and groups. The trainee develops techniques and procedures. For example, the idea that an understanding of the transference situation is central to psychoanalytic work is quite easily transformed and degraded into an empty technical procedure—bookish or intellectual interpretations are dutifully administered but not believed in. I wonder how many supervisors have had the disturbing experience of hearing last week's enjoyable and thought-provoking supervision regurgitated as a technical procedure dutifully administered. Main states quite clearly that he does not know how to prevent this happening. It is worth saying, in passing, that I think it is this sort of problem that leads to some of the misunderstanding between the groups concerning transference interpretations. Often the examples given are examples of these degraded interpretations that parody the idea and transform the "transference interpretation" into a fetish.

This is a very general problem for training and the transmission of knowledge. A patient of mine dreamt of *a man* (identified with me) *who had been away and returned wearing second-hand clothes but claiming they belonged to him.* He was showing his experience of an analyst who offers the supervisor an understanding that is not integrated and so is not felt by the patient to really belong to the analyst.

The presence in the British Psycho-Analytical Society of three groups leads to difficulties that are relevant to the discussion of Main's paper. Membership of a group encourages some of the anti-thought processes that Main describes, and I wonder if this is not the principal reason that he leaves this paper to us as his legacy. Feelings of allegiance to a group, fear of betrayal, the need to champion ideas or protect them, all militate against serious scientific discussion. Members of one group present degraded caricatures of the ideas of another group. Gross generalizations are made that hide the large differences between the individuals in any of the groups. Sometimes, anxieties about group differences lead to insincere praises, to avoid conflict. Groups generate disciples, and, as Main says, it is not easy to suspect ardent followers of one's own ideas as having little capacity for thought or understanding.

CHAPTER TWO

Enquiring into a culture of enquiry

Peter Griffiths & R. D. Hinshelwood

This chapter describes the nature of a culture of enquiry and some of the difficulties that are associated with such a reflective practice. The term was originally coined by Main (1983), the Director of the Cassel Hospital between 1946 and 1976 where he set out to create a model hospital (Main, 1946). Other early experiments in forming therapeutic communities also used similar ideas, such as "analysis of all events" (Clark, 1964) and "reality-confrontation" (Rapaport, 1960).

Though the Cassel Hospital may differ from other therapeutic communities, there is now an increasing consensus that the hallmark of a therapeutic community is a "culture of enquiry" (Main, 1983; Norton, 1992). Main suggested that this was not a particular structure but a living human culture, which enquires into the personal, interpersonal, and intersystem problems that beset the culture, the impulses of its members, and the defences and relations as these are expressed socially (1983). However, Main was also aware

This chapter is a modified version of a paper given in July 1995 to the Conference of the International Society for the Psychoanalytic Study of Organisations.

that organizations can easily become unthinking, un-enquiring monolithic institutions. He particularly had in mind those old and large mental hospitals of the 1940s, as well as aspects of the organization of life in the army (1946). In an earlier paper entitled "Knowledge, Learning and Freedom from Thought", which is reproduced here in chapter one, Main describes how within even well-intentioned organizations there are social and intrapsychic pressures to corrupt or erase thoughtful enquiry.

The observation he wanted to explain was that helping organizations are staffed usually by extremely well-meaning people. Often they develop innovatory projects. However, something so often takes over that, in the course of time, renders that service stale, institutionalized, and seemingly lacking in humanity. He was not content to say that it was merely the inevitable course of time. Instead, he describes how good ideas and theories become mental objects inside the minds of the staff and patients. There, they are then subject to all the curious distortions that occur in the minds of any of us.

Typically, as ideas pass from one person to another, they change their "mental residence", as Main puts it, moving from the thinking areas of the ego into the fixed morality of the ego-ideal and superego. Main (chapter one) suggests that this hierarchical promotion of ideas, from the ego into the superego, can occur in any individual but operates particularly across inter-generational levels. Teaching, knowledge, and learning can be used by the next generation to avoid thoughts, feelings, and the anxieties that accompany them.

All organizations have to solve their problems in practical ways that relate to existing conditions. But once solutions are established, individuals and groups may avoid the strain of uncertainty and anxiety by the relatively mindless pursuit of established practices. Re-thinking their techniques and current problems is given up, as they avoid having to find solutions of their own. Staff use or look for earlier precedents or existing knowledge. Rationales for action become the parroted solutions of earlier learning, of an earlier generation, rather than making the space to re-think them. Useful tools become mere beliefs, sets of never-to-be-questioned, always-to-be-believed rules, which now handicap thought. Above all, the quality of the thinking in the institution subsides into a stale repetition of what is already known and done. Furthermore, this occurs despite the often abundant individual talents of individual people. Tradition attains priority over travail. Fixed procedures emerge out of flexible techniques, and ideas can become moralities (chapter one). Individuals and organizations move from possessing an idea to being possessed by it. The culture of enquiry has to be directed against this ever-encroaching institutionalization.

Norton (1992) has endorsed the term and argues for the role of constant thought in the therapeutic community. He suggests that: "The burden of awareness falls to staff by virtue of their particular role and function in the community. This demands allegiance to the basic principles and ideologies of the therapeutic community, *albeit in a thinking way*" (Norton, 1992, pp. 22–23, emphasis added).

Currently, the therapeutic community embodies the idea that thinking is at risk in helping institutions and needs to be sustained, whatever the specific principles, strategies, and tactics of a particular community. [Manning (1979), following Weber, suggested that all therapeutic communities share, with scientific innovations and social movements, similar characteristics: an early phase of dynamic innovation, often attributable to a few or perhaps one person's enthusiasm; followed by a wider acceptance of the idea, at which point the idea becomes routinized and institutionalized.]

Structural components

The specific kinds of patients and the treatment regime of the Cassel Hospital have been described elsewhere (Griffiths & Pringle, 1997), and it is not necessary to describe this in detail here. However, the principles are based on three interrelated aspects:

1. individual psychoanalytic psychotherapy (Hinshelwood & Skogstad, 1998);

2. psychosocial nursing (Barnes, Griffiths, Ord, & Wells, 1998; Griffiths & Pringle, 1997), which takes place in the context of the therapeutic community;

3. patients working actively with each other in the living commu-
    nity (Drahorad, 1999).

The Cassel Hospital is organized around the work of the day
(point 3 above), and it uses the totality of the daily domestic and
recreational aspects of living, in the service of the therapeutic
work. Reasons for successes and failures in these everyday situations are explored and discussed (Barnes et al., 1998; Griffiths &
Pringle, 1997; Kennedy, Heymans, & Tischler, 1986). This is the
"culture of enquiry".

Specific structures sustain the culture of enquiry. Most important is clarity about the central focus of the work. Extremely clear
models of the inpatient psychotherapy and the psychosocial nursing have been achieved. Against this backdrop, enquiry about any
piece of current practice, successful or unsuccessful, can be made.

Typically, low morale, inefficiency, unpunctuality, absenteeism, and distorted communications between sub-groups as well as
between individuals can be monitored, as well as a multitude of
individual parapraxes and rule-transgressions. However, this is
not an exclusive list.

The formal blueprint of roles and functions is important in the
supervision of the nursing and the community, but there is a need
for other special structural components. One important space for
enquiry and reflection is the key couple (James, 1986): the primary
nurse and the psychotherapist. The subtle, and often blatant, ways
in which patients arouse different conscious and unconscious responses, in members of staff, is familiar, but they may also be an
important indicator of the way a patient is re-enacting patterns of
relating or processing his or her own experiences. The nurse–therapist couple use both formal and informal time to examine their
countertransferences and their working relationship. This may be
supplemented by formal supervision with more senior staff.

In addition, the staff of the whole hospital meet weekly to discuss these countertransferences aroused within the staff as a
whole. These "strains" emerge in terms of individual patients and
incidents and can be married with organizational dynamics within
the staff team and its sub-groups. As well as these components,
there are others devoted to reflective enquiry, notably the interact-

ing system of units [there are separate units within the community for adults, adolescents, and families], and a specific member of staff devoted to action research. These also institute a self-reflective culture of enquiry. (In some ways, this system for enquiry represents what is now formally required in the NHS as clinical audit.)

Freedom from thought and enquiry

However, Main's starting point was that providing formal structural components is not enough. The way the structure is worked and lived, the informal "folkways", also determines the effectiveness of the system. Merely providing a space in the timetable for reflection does not necessarily mean that it will be matched by the individuals' willingness to so enquire of themselves and each other. The critical faculties, embodied in an organizational culture of enquiry, can frequently be corrupted or lost. Like all human endeavour, it runs into trouble. It makes a continual internal demand on staff, as well as patients. Sustained enquiry is taxing and demands some resilience to uncertainty and to one's personal adequacy in the job.

In fact, a complex struggle arises between the use of a reflective space for enquiry and the more defensive shrinking of that space. It may be hijacked for use on other things that are remote from enquiry and may be an expression of a wish to avoid it. The capacity for the organization to become more or less enquiring compares with the dynamics within psychoanalysis that lead the patient to move towards or away from insight.

So, at the heart of the therapeutic community idea there is a dilemma. It was originally an attempt to create an organization that avoided the unhappy institutionalization of patients and staff. To this end, the organization itself—the therapeutic community— must engage in self-reflection to the same extent as its patients and clients. However, the relentless problem never goes away. The system that is designed to establish enquiry can itself be overtaken by just those corrupting influences that undermine enquiry. We have to be prepared for the fact that we encounter the undermining of enquiry itself, and we continually need to enquire into our state of enquiry. This is a unique challenge that could be very stimulating if it were not arduously incessant.

The culture of enquiry needs continually to be set going again and again. It is to those moments when the organization lapses from its continual enquiry that we draw attention in this chapter.

A case study in the culture of a psychoanalytically informed organization

The very nature of the work can often seem to direct us away from attention to the organization and its enquiry. We first describe this in terms of the socio-technical system, and we then go on to describe more specific encroachments on enquiry.

Problems of the socio-technical system

The idea of the socio-technical system (see Trist & Murray, 1993) is that the particular form of work arouses particular difficulties and anxieties. Then the way the work is technically done, and the social relations that grow up, are arranged according to those problems. Particularly where there is a lot of anxiety—and that is true of carer organizations where the "raw material" is anxious other persons— the social relations can be quite significantly determined in the work setting. The study of a nursing service by Menzies (1959) is well known (see also Miller & Gwynne, 1972). Those determining effects are often unconsciously driven and maintained, which makes them elusive to grasp.

The socio-technical system of the Cassel is an application of psychoanalysis. Inevitably, therefore, the couple forms a unique reference point in practice and thinking—for example, between patient and therapist, between patient and nurse, and between nurse and therapist. The patients themselves are intent on an individualistic outcome. This often derives from their experience of a health care system in which one-to-one working is often privileged, in rhetoric if not in reality. Their wish for one-to-one work is also enhanced by factors in their early developmental history and narcissistic preoccupations at the core of their personality. Thus, invariably what happens between the pair is given the greatest status by the patients and the institution employing psychoanalytic psychotherapy.

Nurses also come to the Cassel often motivated by a wish to undertake one-to-one work with patients. Therapists are trained in individual psychoanalytic psychotherapy, and many nurses commence personal therapy, often individual psychoanalytic psychotherapy, while working at the hospital. Even group therapy prioritizes the individual as the object of any outcome achievement, and all forms of thinking about a care institution go back inevitably to psychoanalytic ideas derived from the pair. Hence, needy patients in search of the ideal pair come to the hospital and find nurses and therapists in search of individual patients (Denford & Griffiths, 1993; Mason, 1994).

In a psychoanalytically informed therapeutic community like the Cassel, it is perhaps not surprising therefore that the focus of understanding concerning emotional experience is to be found in the space between the pair. Writing about psychoanalytic institutions in general, Eisold concluded that "The primacy of the involvement of the pair generates greater ambivalence at best and resentment at worst about the constraints of organisational life; the organisation is seen more easily as intrusive and becomes more readily the object of attack" (Eisold, 1994, p. 793).

In the minds of its members, a hospital institution tends to become reduced to a set of relationships and affiliations based on the pair. Therefore, inevitably, just from the character of the work, enquiry is drawn to the emotional space between the pair. Enquiry into broader aspects of the organization tends progressively to be restricted.

We would claim that this pressure to view the pair as the focal organization to be enquired into is endemic in any institution that seeks to help people, including the therapeutic community. In terms of the socio-therapeutic system, the technical demand to achieve a change in the individual person skews the thinking of the organization away from wider organizational issues and dynamics. Above all, subjectively it feels natural to the members of the organization to focus on individuals.

However, this is not the only threat that the culture of enquiry has to combat. There are other, more specific processes that infiltrate enquiry.

Specific methods of closing enquiry

Experience within the Cassel Hospital demonstrates many ways in which the reflective space for enquiry can be closed off. Menzies' (1959) descriptions of a nursing service in a general hospital pinpointed a series of "defensive techniques" that protected the individuals from disturbing experiences in their work. In that instance, young nurses were in daily and prolonged contact with people who were in pain, mutilated, and dying. If the nurses related too closely and emotionally with the suffering patients, they could suffer greatly themselves. Defensive techniques had grown up, in the way the work was practised, that kept nurses at a safe emotional distance from their patients. Similar social systems of defence against emotional experience have been identified in the professional practices of other care workers (Woodhouse & Pengelly, 1991).

Similarly in a therapeutic community, practices can grow up that create a distance for staff (and patients) from too much enquiry where emotional awareness would be demanded. These phenomena arising from a "culture of anti-enquiry" are used and mobilized as defences against individuals' experiences within the hospital, which contains pain and despair (Armstrong, 1992). However, as with the phenomena Menzies described, they often increase anxiety and confusion as they require a denial of some aspects of reality and so deny any realistic processing of the experience by understanding it.

The packed timetable

Much of the daily timetable is a plethora of meetings, each beginning as another ends. While they are seen as part of the daily work and regarded as "containing for patients and staff", they are often embedded in unquestioned assumptions. The meetings themselves often mirror the timetable, with an impossibly packed agenda. The ensuing rush obviates thought and enquiry and avoids painful anxiety, particularly about adequacy to perform the task. Perhaps this is a defence against the feelings of guilt, failure, and depression that arise inevitably from the unfulfilled idealized wishful expectations of the patients, and from the staff's own idealized reparative motives (Meinrath & Roberts, 1982; Roberts, 1994).

The projection of despair

A similar avoidance is accomplished by the emphasis on how difficult the patients are—hopeless cases who are at the end of the road. In reflecting the patients' perceptions that treatment is often their last chance, and so their last hope, staff can feel relieved that anything they do is better than nothing, and so inadequacy no longer feels relevant. The problem is that such cultivated despair can numb curiosity, by both patients and staff, about the real possibilities for some patients.

Paranoid explanations/interpretations

Staff regularly use phrases such as "I felt attacked", "You were obviously attacked", or "That's an attack on the institution" about patients' verbal utterances and behaviours. At these times, the emphasis concentrates on how unpleasant, or monstrous, the patients are. Their inherent malevolence is assumed. An enquiry into the real possibilities is obliterated. While such comments are seemingly critical and devaluing of patients, in truth they often reflect the staff's vulnerability. Patients feel aggrieved, deprived, frustrated, or disappointed (especially disappointed with staff), and staff are vulnerable to feeling disappointed in themselves. Paranoid attitudes evade the tension that arises because patients may both attack and at the same time appreciate gratefully, and need help to sort out their confusion. Tension in staff because they may at times feel sadistic while also wishing the best for their patients may also be evaded by such attitudes.

Last-minutism

An often crisis-led, fire-fighting atmosphere prevails. Short-term needs predominate, often exacerbated recently by so-called "business" pressures. A just-in-time, last-minutism pervades. It cramps space for reviewing current experience, or for developing a vision for the future. Crisis management can at times be thrilling, and the excitement overtakes planning and reflective thought. The hospital business plan tends to state what the hospital does, less of what it might become. In a hospital relatively recently marked down for closure (Robinson, 1994), anxiety about survival of the Cassel might understandably be avoided by obliterating the future itself. However, at least as important is the avoidance in this of the problematic future of the often-hopeless patients. Time can in Bion's terms become for the hospital, as for many patients, a "time-less present" (Turquet, 1985).

"Tribalism"

Structurally separated into three units (adolescent, adult, fami-lies), the Cassel Hospital invites an institutional schism, when separateness drifts into opposition between the clinical units. Each of the three consultants in charge jealously preserves his or her own unit's autonomy. Each team can function as a "tribe" address-ing only its own interests. Though censured as anti-communal, it is at the same time sustained, as if no one can change it. This tribalism impoverishes enquiry about difficult work, because it comfortingly locates anxiety, and especially the despair about such work, in another unit.

An example of this was a meeting (of senior clinicians from each unit) held at the end of each week. A ritualized agenda was followed in which each unit gave a rote description of their clin-ical issues and concerns and to which others paid respectful dis-interest. Acknowledging this dysfunctional routine, it was agreed to re-define the purpose of this meeting as a more open discussion, to favour more creative thought on issues that affect each or all of the units. It was then striking that this change brought discomfort and vulnerability to the members of the meeting, as the real effects of one unit upon another had to be faced. Attempts to further re-define the meeting, or end early each week, were a regular feature for some time after.

Interprofessional rivalries

As with the "tribal" rivalries between the units, so are there rivalries between the disciplines. Differences concerning status, pay, working rationales, practices, and the knowledge and as-sumptions that underpin them are all too obvious. Stokes (1994) has written of the difficulties of multidisciplinary team working and the often confusing and conflicted picture that presents when different staff groups mobilize different basic assumption mentali-ties for sophisticated use, in the pursuit of their work. The pairing role of therapist and patient may often be at odds with the depend-ent or fight–flight, reality-orientated role of the nurse in the work of the community. The question for any institution is how to medi-ate and live with inequalities, jealousy, and rivalry. Unlike the units, tribal division is not usually an option. Multidisciplinary team working is a badge of the Cassel Hospital. However, it can become a dogma and therefore itself difficult to question: interdis-ciplinary conflict may be avoided, hidden, and cloaked by a superegoish demand to present a "containing" united front, so that patient splitting does not occur. In addition, a particular focus on the state of another unit's staff members, or of the relations be-tween the unit teams, can itself become an avoidance from explor-ing very unhappy relations between the disciplines, across or within the units.

Interdisciplinary rivalries are stoked up when patients empha-size differences between them. Therapists are often perceived as providing the hopeful thinking and feeling space, and they are regularly and consistently present for patients, in a one-to-one manner. On the other hand, nurses are felt to be present in an inconsistent and consistent manner, through shift working and taking days off in lieu of emergency hours. Patients have to compete with other patients for the nurse's time. Nurses are often perceived by the patients, and therapists, as responsible for the patients and all their needs, during all the community life when the patient is not seeing the therapist. Patients often look with great dependency towards the nurse for this nursing. In fact, psychosocial nursing is often quite confrontative, in terms of making patients aware of both their daily responsibilities and the effects of their actions on others; in this way, it not only confronts but frustrates patients at a deep level. The upshot can be a dangerous split between a sympathetic and understanding therapist on the one hand and a confrontative, controlling nurse on the other. Often, the split confirms therapists as the guardians of the reflective function, while nurses "merely" react and bustle. Anna Dartington (1993) has drawn attention to this dynamic and the way in which nurses, dynamically, are left to often hold onto the un-thinking space for many other professionals. Interdisciplinary differences in work practices could be enriching were they not a cleavage that allows a solution and an evasion of the tension between careful listening and firm boundaries.

Pseudomutualism

Another response to the painful inequalities between staff is the escape into a pseudomutual world, in which true differentiation is avoided, in a sentimental egalitarianism. In such a culture, enquiry and development is seen as an irrelevance, at times a nuisance, and moreover a threat. Gustafson (1976) has suggested that in such a culture, anyone questioning the rationales of the culture will either be marginalized or be promoted into a position of impotence.

The abuse of psychoanalysis as a mean of inhibiting enquiry

Four processes that close off enquiry involve the use of psychoanalytic ideas themselves. In this sense, they pervert knowledge rather than simply deny it. Furthermore, they comprise phenomena comparable to descriptions by Joseph (1989) and Steiner (1993).

Ritual interpretations

Reiterated psychoanalytic insights can be preferred to what is unknown about the patient. For example, staff holidays, absences, and leavings can stir up patients' earlier experiences of loss and abandonment. Named at one time as "the usual suspects", they can be ritualistically invoked as explanations for a multitude of largely unexplored individual and organizational symptoms. This is not to suggest that they are not unimportant events, merely that their significance is overplayed before their effects have been explored and are better known. The absence of anger in the community is invariably thought of as evidence of repressed anger; overt anger is a denial of sadness; overt sadness is false because it excludes ambivalence; and so forth. Subtly, people can claim the wisdom of a supervisor through such incantations, often sympathetically intoned, so that what looks like thinking is in fact a rather superior distance from enquiring into a distress, which is thereby rendered silent.

The corporate individual

At other times, the state of the hospital can be addressed in terms of individual mechanisms as described by psychoanalysis. Transposed to the organizational level, unconscious phantasies discovered in individuals are re-found as generalized corporate entities. For instance, the facile discovery of mother and father figures in senior staff obliterates a real understanding of how authority is being used or misused. Such ideas can often then be felt as imposed on the individual members, and this strikes out the possibility of struggling to recognize the real attributes and problems of individuals homogenized at the organizational level.

Competitive interpretation

In many meetings, the temptation to make interpretations of a group or individual kind overtakes a number of people at any one time. A competition is risked. Serial interpretations, in which each interpretation tends to interpret the one before, lead to or create a kind of league table of interpreters striving for the "Nobel Prize winning interpretation" (Main, 1975b). There appears to be little true insight gained from these attempts to understand. One effect is that real work and decision making grinds to a halt in what might be characterized as a "paralysis of analysis". At that point, with frustration mounting at the inauthenticity of the discussions, a clinching intervention will describe all the interpretations as if it were "play". The implication is that it should be stopped in favour of the real business of clinical work. Again, the agony of not knowing, and of being at sea, is momentarily submerged in the competition or in a return to the individual in the "clinic".

Competition may be useful to stimulate striving, but in this instance it appears more in the service of achieving a pre-eminence and projection of inadequacy (or despair) into those whose prior interpretations have been usurped. Real understanding is perverted in this instance into a commodity for asserting superior knowledge and avoiding everyone's uncertainty.

Discipline

The flexible balance between social control and understanding is easily disturbed in a therapeutic institution. Often, the psychotherapist's authority is inappropriately required to assert a form of social control over patients behaving defiantly. Interpretations degenerate into criticism and are felt as fierce or desperate demands for patients to reform rather than to understand. Psychoanalysis is removed, by excess anxiety, from a role of enquiring and understanding the individual and his or her organizational context, to become a superego for the individual.

In these last four processes, psychoanalytic interpretations themselves can be specifically recruited to shut down thought and enquiry of a psychoanalytic kind. These obviously obstructive ways of using psychoanalysis are reminiscent of the perversion of truth which so characterizes the personality disorders of the patients that the Cassel Hospital typically treats. Hence, these features in the hospital may well be linked to the specific task that the hospital undertakes with them.

Conclusion

We have described many manoeuvres, and in the main these are unconscious. Nevertheless, in the relatively safe environment of a training seminar, nurses have been able to describe some of the anxieties that they feel are inherent in the nature of their work: bizarre thoughts and dreams; fear of failure; empathizing with pain; recognizing one's own madness, exposure, and vulnerability; fears of destructiveness and being destroyed; nameless dread; fear of persecution; and fear of the recognition, in the large group, of one's own madness.

Part of the problem is that to give up these defensive techniques and rationalizations means questioning and embarking on a journey into the unknown, usually an unknown of intolerable and perhaps fantastical anxieties. To address these processes consciously within the institution requires giving up an important assumption: that emotional experience is strictly limited within one's own skin, or that of another—the pair. Unconsciously determined assumptions (such as the priority of the pair) form the core of a social system of defence. It is a system that protects against the specific pain and horror of the work. The latter include, among many others, sexual and physical abuse, infanticide, murder and murderous feelings, and violence to self.

A psychoanalytically informed organization clearly has the possibility of understanding this interplay between anxieties, social defences, and the "freedom" from thought. However, we have described how that sophistication can always be turned into a sophisticated method of undermining enquiry and sticking closely to the already known.

We are not, however, helpless in the face of these problems. We can turn to the practice of psychoanalysis itself. There, the non-use of the treatment for insight is known as the transference. Interestingly, it is analysis of the transference, *par excellence* (those processes that similarly encroach on the analytic enquiry), that reveals the unknown that is being fought off. It is likely to be little different in organizations. Those impasses in organizational change that we might so bemoan are of the highest interest just because they conceal (and thus reveal) the points of maximum anxiety and pain within the work. One could take heart that we have such indicators of the place where anxiety is most concentrated, and thus most needs containing.

This chapter was born out of the ongoing enquiry of the Cassel Hospital's structure and culture. Though the chapter is in some ways already dated, and we must stick with this already known, it is in itself an illustrative record of reflection that went on at one point in our culture of enquiry. We claim that this is the stuff of therapeutic community practice. The primary task includes not just enquiry into what is happening, but enquiry into what is happening to our abilities to go on enquiring.

CHAPTER THREE

Internal and external reality: enquiring into their interplay in an inpatient setting

Wilhelm Skogstad

In this chapter, I focus on the relationship between working on the internal reality and the external reality of patients in inpatient treatment at the Cassel Hospital. The hospital setting provides a space in external reality in which aspects of a patient's internal reality can be played out and worked with through reflective enquiry and containment. I hope to be able to show that the combination of working on internal and external aspects of a patient's pathology in a joint effort of therapy and nursing staff can have powerful therapeutic effects and can act against the strong regressive pull that patients experience in a hospital setting.

This chapter is a revised version of a paper given at the Furtbachkrankenhaus in Stuttgart, Germany, on 12 November 1999, and was awarded the Tom Main Memorial Prize in January 2000.

The hospital as a therapeutic institution

In psychoanalytic psychotherapy with severely disturbed patients, we hope to improve a person's internal and external functioning. We try to achieve changes in the patient's internal world and thereby not only to improve his or her emotional well-being, but to influence the way in which the internal world impinges on his or her functioning in the real world of relationships, work, and every-day life. In order to do this, we need to work on the complicated interchange between the internal and external world. For example, we need to watch carefully how parts of the external world are filled with projections, and aspects of the internal world are thereby got rid of; similarly, we need to recognize how aspects of internal reality are evaded by avoiding parts of external reality that represent them.

However, there is always the risk that instead of helping patients deal with their internal and external world, one colludes with them in creating a refuge in which the disturbing aspects of their internal and external world need not be faced and no real change takes place. O'Shaughnessy (1992) describes such situations in analysis as "enclaves" and "excursions". Such collusive manoeuvres can be seen as enactments of what Steiner (1993) calls "psychic retreats". He describes these retreats as "states of mind in which the patient is stuck, cut off and out of reach" (p. 2), providing him or her "with an area of relative peace and protection from strain when meaningful contact with the analyst is experienced as threatening." (p. 1). One of the features of the retreat is that:

> the avoidance of contact with the analyst is at the same time an avoidance of contact with reality. The retreat then serves as an area of the mind where reality does not have to be faced, where phantasy and omnipotence can exist unchecked and where anything is permitted. [p. 3]

While this risk is present in any psychotherapy, I see a particular danger of creating an unhelpful refuge in an inpatient setting. The whole setting may become an enclave in which the patient is removed from the reality of ordinary relationships, tasks, and responsibilities and can avoid not only external difficulties but the corresponding aspects of his or her internal reality. The removal from outside reality in an inpatient setting is often longed for by patients, reflecting their hatred of reality and of the frustration and guilt that facing reality brings with it. Such an approach may, therefore, foster an unhelpfully regressive culture in which patients and staff can collude in the omnipotent phantasy that reality, ordinary limitations, and responsibilities can be avoided and infantile demands can be met. The institution as a whole may come to stand for the retreat in the patient's mind to which he or she can withdraw.

Main (1946), from a slightly different theoretical perspective, wrote about the traditional hospital setting:

> Within such a setting, health and stability are too often bought at the excessive price of desocialization. Sooner or later the patient, alone and unsupported, must face the difficult task of returning to the society in which he became unstable, and there regain social integration and a daily sense of values and purpose. This task is no light one for a desocialized man, however healthy he may have become. The design of a hospital as a social retreat also ignores positive therapeutic forces—the social support and emotional opportunities that are granted in spontaneously structured communities. [pp. 7–8)]

Main concluded that the hospital itself must become a "therapeutic institution" (p. 8). He saw as particularly anti-therapeutic the mutual projective processes of staff and patients in which "the helpful and the helpless meet and put pressure on each other to act not only in realistic but in fantastic collusion". Staff and patients unconsciously require each other to be helpless and helpful and thus become "to some extent creatures of each other" (1975a, p. 103). In such a mutually collusive situation, patients are prevented from reintrojecting healthier aspects of themselves and may even give up capacities they currently possess. For the institution to be more therapeutic, he thought that "the daily life of the community must be related to real tasks, truly relevant both to the needs and aspirations of the small society of the hospital and to the larger society in which it is set" (1946, p. 8). Later he suggested that a "total culture of enquiry" (1983) was necessary in which *all* aspects of treatment and *all* relationships within it were open to enquiry.

In inpatient treatment the setting is constituted by all the thera-
pies and the social environment together. It is, therefore, a matter
of the *whole* institution and not just of the psychotherapy within
it, whether the setting is therapeutic or not. Treating the psychotherapy as independent from the social reality of the hospital
would be equivalent in outpatient therapy to ignoring important
aspects of the transference relationship, such as the way the patient
deals with the setting and its boundaries. Even a very capable
therapist who can analyse the patient's defences without getting
drawn too much into collusive enactments will, therefore, not be
able to prevent a powerful anti-therapeutic influence of the whole
institution.

What is necessary, therefore, is:

• to create a setting that is not a refuge removed from ordinary
  reality but a place where internal and external reality and the
  interchange between them can be fully explored;

• in the therapeutic work with patients, to address the whole of
  the transference as it develops to different parts and people
  within the institution (Hinshelwood & Skogstad, 1998), as well
  as to the institution as a whole (Denford & Griffiths, 1993);

• to create a culture in which interpersonal, group and institutional dynamics of patients and staff can be openly enquired
  into.

The work of the day:
internal and external reality

In the majority of patients who come for inpatient treatment, there
has been a breakdown in their capacity to deal with everyday life.
Kennedy (1997), from the Cassel Hospital, suggests that in these
patients,

> the things most people do without thinking—such as sleeping,
> washing, eating, eating meals with others, as well as more
> interpersonal functions such as cooking, cleaning, caring for
> others, receiving care, and being involved in social activities—

are charged with emotion and conflict, to the degree that there is a breakdown in the continuity and consistency of daily life. The life of the day is not "held together". [p. 20]

To put it differently, areas and functions of everyday life are filled with disturbing projections and the mental work that is necessary to digest these experiences, what Kennedy calls the "work of the day", cannot be done.

As inpatient psychotherapy may allow many of these tasks of everyday life to be avoided and left to others, there is a *risk* of a refuge being built in which no real therapeutic work takes place. The inpatient setting, however, offers also a *chance*, if the opportunity of the living-in situation is used to work directly on the patients' difficulties with their external reality and the correspondent internal aspects. In that case, patients' particular pathologies and transference dynamics may simultaneously be worked on in psychotherapy and in (almost) a real life situation. The focus on external reality may also help to avoid the development of an unhelpful regressive refuge.

This is the approach developed at the Cassel Hospital. It not only offers patients, through psychoanalytic psychotherapy, a way of thinking about their inner life in the context of a transference relationship, but also introduces real-life tasks in which they will encounter and be able to work on anxieties and conflicts relevant to their core pathologies. This is the arena of the nurses and their particular work known as "psychosocial nursing" (Barnes, 1968; Griffiths & Leach, 1998; Griffiths & Pringle, 1997). Here, too, work takes place within a transference relationship, through containment of anxieties and on the basis of psychodynamic understanding; however, in contrast to the boundaried setting of psychotherapy, this happens in a more direct, task-oriented contact with less strict boundaries. In patients with severe personality disorders, actions so often become the currency of communication because of the severe problems in their capacity to symbolize and to think about feelings. Thus, in the psychosocial work actions are taken as a basis for thought with the aim of moving from mindless action to thoughtful activity (Griffiths & Hinshelwood, 1997).

The space for doing this work of acting and reflecting on the actions is provided by the everyday life of the hospital. Patients are involved to quite a degree in the everyday running of the hospital and the patient community, and they depend on each other and not only on staff for the functioning of their daily lives. These areas of real life provide spaces for enquiring into and working on the internal reality of patients.

For example, all patient areas of the hospital are looked after by designated work groups consisting each of a few patients and a nurse. Looking after one's living areas is much more than a burdensome activity within external reality. The concrete container of the hospital draws powerful transferences onto itself, often of quite a negative kind. It may be experienced like a mother's body, towards which destructive attacks are launched. The messiness in the patients' minds and the hatred of their own bodies are often reflected in the messy and neglectful way they treat their surroundings. In challenging this, staff come up against powerful internal dynamics but may gradually enable the patient to introject a more caring attitude towards themselves and their environment.

The feeding of the patients takes a central place in the everyday life of the community, and there are a number of different work groups concerned with the ordering and storing of food and the planning and preparation of meals (C. Flynn, 1993). Food and feeding are highly charged with emotions and phantasies, not just in patients with eating disorders. Envy and hatred of the feeding mother or breast, insatiable greed, and the inability to allow oneself to be fed and satisfied or to feed and give to others may all come up in this context and have wider implications, as they reflect not only literal feeding but emotional feeding as well.

The support of patients who are struggling is seen as a mutual responsibility of the patients. They are therefore encouraged to find their own resources and help each other instead of turning only to staff or withdrawing. This culture fosters in patients the capacity for care and concern for themselves and each other and constantly addresses the obstacles to that capacity. These often lie in severe narcissistic problems: asking for or accepting help may be experienced as a major threat to one's omnipotence, and a patient's suffering self may be treated with severe contempt by him/herself. It can often be through the concern that others show for them that patients become able to identify with a more caring attitude towards themselves.

Responsibility is a key issue in this culture, and the way responsibility is avoided is an important focus in the work with patients (Griffiths & Hinshelwood, 1997). The capacity to take responsibility involves tolerating feelings of guilt and is linked with the depressive position (Klein, 1935). It also involves the realization that one's feelings, though influenced by others, are of one's own making and that one's feelings and actions have an effect on other people. Taking that into account may include making amends for emotional or material damage that one has done. A severe obstacle to such a capacity is a very harsh and tyrannical superego, which leads to persecuting guilt and a crushing sense of failure. These depressive and persecutory anxieties may be evaded internally by denial and projection or by withdrawal into the psychic retreat, and externally by giving up ordinary activity altogether.

An ordinary inpatient setting may actually reinforce the internal and external evasion of responsibility by permitting or even encouraging patients to give up responsibility, thus allowing them to remain internally in their retreat. *Real* responsibilities with a mutual interdependence of patients on a practical and emotional level is therefore seen as crucial for treatment. What patients do or don't do in community life has an effect in the real world on others; for example, not long ago, problems in the supper team led to a situation where no supper was cooked and people had to make do with sandwiches.

Confronting patients with these mutual effects in their practical and emotional reality is an important part of the staff's work and can help patients move out of their stuck pathological position. It requires a constant enquiring into and addressing of the quality of relationships of patients with each other and with staff. An important reflective space for this work of enquiry is provided by daily meetings of the patients of a unit, together with their nurses and the unit consultant.

In order for the work to be truly therapeutic, this arena of the nursing work needs to be brought together with that of the psychotherapy, through an understanding, first of all, in the minds of the workers and through their containment of powerful feelings. In the following sections, I draw upon clinical material to illustrate how the internal reality of a patient may be played out and worked with in the psychotherapy setting as well as in the external environment and everyday work within the wider hospital setting and how this setting offers a space to enquire into the interplay between internal and external reality.

A world filled with projections

The first case example shows how part of ordinary reality may for a patient be filled with terrifying projections and thereby become unmanageable, and how therapeutic work can be done simultaneously in the arenas of psychotherapy and psychosocial nursing.

"Barbara" is a female adolescent who was severely sexually abused as a child. Like all patients, she is required to go home regularly over the weekends in order to remain linked with her outside reality and prevent her from becoming overdependent on the institution. After a while it was discovered that, although she left for the weekend, she never went to her own flat but stayed instead with friends. When confronted, she said that she just could not go there but didn't seem to know why. It was decided that her primary nurse should accompany her home during the week to help her get back into the flat. However, when they came near the home, Barbara ran away in panic. Later, when they actually entered the flat, the patient was overcome by terror. This continued, but even though Barbara never managed to stay, she refused to consider giving up her flat. Her nurse, although patient, experienced helplessness, despair, and anger and could only manage these visits with a lot of support from the team.

In the first weeks of her individual therapy, Barbara screamed on the way to the therapist's room as if being tortured and was unable to enter the room. After a while, she could enter but only stayed for 5 or 10 minutes. Gradually the time she stayed increased, but she turned her body away from her therapist and remained silent. The therapist felt helpless, paralysed, and hardly able to think but also felt invited by the patient to intrude into her with aggressive or abusive comments. The patient thus enacted a sadomasochistic position in which she was stuck, and by physically and emotionally turning away she seemed to prevent herself from getting any help.

In the hospital, Barbara held the job of a community chairperson. In this role, she, together with a fellow patient, chaired meetings of all the inpatients and had a central role within the therapeutic community, working closely with some patients and with the community nurses who helped her in this role. She fulfilled this role competently and was particularly keen and able to help others think and speak about their difficulties and get help in this way. This, of course, made her acutely aware of her own inability to speak about herself or get out of her sadomasochistic situation.

Gradually a change occurred. She began to stay in her therapy sessions and was at times able to speak and think in her sessions. She started to make hints to her therapist about the violent, abusive contact she had had with her former boyfriend with whom she had lived in her flat, and she started to talk about her sexual abuse as a child. The therapist had more of a sense of contact and of, albeit distressing, life in the sessions. Barbara, instead of being mindless, now seemed to experience pain in the session; she started to have tormenting flashbacks which she hadn't had before and, for a while, felt quite suicidal. On the level of her outside life she started to consider giving up her flat and looking for a new one.

What had happened? Initially parts of external reality—the flat and the therapy room—were filled with undigested psychic material, unconscious memories of abuse, and phantasies of violence. Through this process these rooms became dangerous and threatening, had to be avoided, and, if entered, caused extreme anxiety, while her mind had become empty and thinking could not take place. Some of the disturbing feelings had to be contained by the therapist and the nurse. The patient seemed stuck in a position where she was terrified of abuse while also inviting it and was unable to let go of a view of her workers as abusers. The therapist worked with this enactment in the context of the session, while the nurse explored the patient's stuck position in the concrete world of her flat, not only encouraging her to do something but doing it *with* her and tolerating frustration and irritation. Their containment gradually helped the patient to become able to hold more of her disturbing mental content in her mind and make initial steps out of her stuck sadomasochistic position. She started, to some degree, to think about her experiences, to have memories, and to experience mental suffering. At the same time, she was, with help, functioning in the real world of responsibilities as a community chairperson. There, the nurses working alongside her observed the extent to which she projected all her disturbance into other patients whom she helped and encouraged. They frequently challenged her about this, and this gradually enabled her to see aspects of herself in others, such as the inviting of abuse and rejecting of help. She also realized how other patients were being helped and, through intro-jection of such more benign relationships, gained some capacity to think and speak about herself.

This case illustrates that the same internal problem may be enacted and a similar transference dynamic may develop in the confined setting of the individual psychotherapy *and* in the work on the reality within the realm of psychosocial nursing work. It can be worked with in both arenas, interpretatively in one and more practically in the other. The need for the workers to contain dis-turbing feelings in themselves and to work with strong resistances in the patients is present in both arenas. It also demonstrates that work in the realm of practical tasks can help patients function in some areas of their life and thereby prevent them from regressing severely on *all* levels. It can also help patients detect aspects of themselves in others and re-introject them.

Steps out of a retreat

I have argued that in a traditional hospital setting the whole hospi-tal may come to stand in the patient's mind for a psychic retreat into which he or she can withdraw to an extent that prevents therapeutic work. On the other hand, combining work on a pa-tient's internal reality with work on his or her external reality and focusing on the interplay of these may be particularly effective in

helping a patient make steps out of his or her retreat. I would like
to illustrate this with another case example.

"Peter" is an extremely schizoid man who feels inferior and
without any social capacities. His father left the family when he
was 2 years old, and he has lived with grandmother, mother,
and a younger sister ever since. He has had hardly any contact
outside, the only friend he ever had having moved away when
he was 12, but he has also been withdrawn within this all-
female family. Having felt treated very differently as a child
than his sister, he has always felt he had no right to exist. He
once thought of a film in which a mother had to choose one of
her children to go to a concentration camp, and he felt certain
that his mother would have chosen him. Coming to the Cassel,
he was terrified of the social contacts and felt unable to share a
room with anyone. He fled home in panic when this appeared
to be necessary, and for a while he could only manage a short-
ened week within the hospital.

In his therapy sessions he seemed extremely cautious, kept the
therapist at great distance, and spoke in a highly intellectual
way. Whenever the therapist talked to him about his state of
mind, he became anxious and distressed, breathing heavily as if
he were suffocating. He seemed to experience the therapist as
barging violently into his mind. The therapist became extremely cautious and hardly dared to challenge his extremely
restricted way of relating to her. She found herself talking in a
similarly intellectual way. Thus for a while he seemed to suc-
ceed in completely controlling the therapist's mind and the
distance between them. When the therapist became aware of
this and started to interpret more of his anxiety and evasion, he
brought two dreams to his sessions within a week. One was of
*a window that came closer and closer to his face and covered it with
cellophane in a frightening way.* The other was of *his bedroom in the
hospital being full of poisonous insects which he couldn't touch for
fear of being poisoned; full of terror, he was standing with his back to
the wall.* The therapist spoke to him about his terror of being
suffocated by her if he comes close to her and the fear that
dangerously poisonous thoughts from her could enter his mind.

At the beginning of the following session, he took his glasses off and expressed a wish to feel less constrained. In the course of the session he talked about some of his painful experience of a bleak and lonely childhood in which he had felt disgusting and despised; unlike before, the therapist felt moved by his account.

In the hospital community, he was working as one of the managers in the servery. This involved cleaning the kitchen and ordering cleaning material and collecting the ordered items, together with his nurse. He was meticulous in his work and competent in managing it but was full of contempt for these mundane tasks and completely out of his depth when it came to relating. When other patients did not turn up on time to the work group and the nurse asked him what he wanted to do about it, he pressed her to go up and get them; he seemed too terrified of entering anyone's private space. The servery was often messy because some patients left their cereals everywhere, which angered him, but he felt unable to confront them about it. Also, he never joined the cup of tea and chat with the others at the end of the work group.

A new bin needed to be ordered, and the nurse wanted to choose one with him out of a brochure. Quickly he made a choice of his own which the nurse found unsuitable and told him so. Peter reacted by snatching the brochure from her in a sudden violent outburst of fury and contempt that left the nurse feeling shaken. A team discussion helped her understand how Peter felt in need of omnipotent control and experienced her independent thought as a violent intrusion. She started challenging more vigorously his rigid control, even though she often feared a violent reaction. She also made a point of conveying clearly to him how much she valued his contribution in their work, which she genuinely felt. In a regular weekly meeting with a senior member of the ancillary staff, Peter and the nurse discussed the state of the servery, and the patient gradually discovered that his thoughts and suggestions were taken seriously even though they were not always accepted.

While initially he could only be close to a patient who confirmed his paranoid view of the hospital, within the work of the servery he gradually and cautiously started approaching other patients and accepting his nurse working with him. He had refused a home visit before admission and for a long time afterwards, terrified of any intrusion into his home. Eventually he agreed to his nurse and another patient visiting him at home. At this visit, he was very moved and told them that he had not had anyone visiting him for 12 years, and he cried desperately.

This patient's unconscious phantasies of close relationships are of an extreme kind: either of him invading an object and being suffocated within it, or of others violently intruding into him. He tries to defend himself against such experience by being extremely controlling within himself and towards others. If he cannot fully control the others, he reacts with violent anger, which he is also frightened of. While this was played out within his therapy and gradually interpreted there, it was also enacted in the everyday situation of the hospital setting, such as in the servery work group or in his strongly defended distance from others. The lessening of his persecutory anxieties in the transference through interpretation went hand in hand with a similar development in the community setting, where he became more able to share and make contact. In both settings, one could see him, at times, come out of his psychic and social retreat, leading to livelier interactions but also to pain and anxiety. Of course, he would then retreat again—for example, when, the day after his home visit, he dismissed the whole experience—but gradually he came out more often and for more prolonged periods of time. This happened not only as a result of the interpretations and containment in his therapy, but because his nurse was able to understand his fears, contain her own anxiety of his violence, and challenge him while retaining sympathy for him. This enabled the patient to introject an object that was more benign and containing and was less frightened of his violence.

The nurse–therapist couple and the internal couple

The two different arenas—the psychotherapy and the nursing work—are represented for the patient by his or her two primary workers: the psychotherapist and the primary nurse. Each patient is therefore faced with a couple, and this is reflected in each of the hospital units with the couple of the consultant and the senior nurse. Patients will be curious about and sensitive to the actual quality of the relationship of their therapeutic couple and the unit's couple but, moreover, will experience them in the light of their own internal oedipal couple. Patients may, for example, feel jealous and furious for being excluded from their phantasized excited intercourse or feel extremely threatened by any link they might make. The patients may, therefore, actively try to keep them apart. Given the tendency for severe splitting in patients with personality disorders, the different workers may come to represent different split-off parts in the patient's mind which need to be prevented from coming together. These dynamics can then have a powerful effect on the reality of the relationship between nurse and therapist, which therefore needs careful observing, particularly as it in turn influences the patient's state of mind.

I have described elsewhere (Hinshelwood & Skogstad, 1998) how the capacity of this therapeutic couple to bring split-off parts together in *their* minds can enable the patient to introject a more integrated version of him/herself in his or her own mind. The same applies on a group level, for the unit couple of senior nurse and consultant. An important part of the setting, whose aim it is to enable this integration within a patient's therapeutic couple, is a regular joint supervision of a patient's nurse and therapist through a senior couple such as the consultant and senior nurse. Enquiring into the nature and dynamics of staff relationships with patients and with each other, which is done also in other structures, can give essential clues for understanding the aspects of patients' internal worlds which are being played out.

I would like to use another clinical example to show how a patient's internal couple can be projected into the therapeutic couple and into different parts of the hospital and can have an actual effect on the reality of the people concerned. The recognition of this process can open ways to useful therapeutic work.

"Jane" first broke down as an adolescent when she was together with a violent and abusive boyfriend. Subsequently, she had an abusive relationship with a psychologist who saw her professionally but seduced her into joint drinking and misuse of drugs. Before admission, as a young adult, she made increasingly serious suicide attempts by taking potentially lethal overdoses, a kind of Russian roulette which she is fascinated by. She frequently gets drunk, burns her skin, or starves herself. Her parents tried unsuccessfully to abort her and appeared to be staying together only because of her. She portrays the mother of her childhood as depressed and violent and physically and emotionally abusive towards her, and her father as a loving man who was very close to her and the only one who understood her. While presenting herself as soft and pretty, she can be very dismissive and even cruel.

In the patient community, she aligned herself with an overtly soft but controlling and schizoid man, "Peter", and they seemed to confirm and support each other's paranoid version of the hospital. She shared a room with another patient, "Ann", who self-harmed occasionally by violently punching the wall with her fist. Jane and Ann also worked together as chairpersons of their "firm" meetings.* One day, Ann revealed that she had bought a small knife; she initially agreed to hand it in but then refused to do so. Their mutual nurse, maybe naively, was not worried that Ann might do something harmful with the knife. Jane, however, got very frightened when she heard this, and then very aggressive, calling Ann hatefully a "psychopath". When her nurse reminded her of her own violence towards herself, she just shouted at her. Even after Ann had handed in the knife, Jane showed an extreme mixture of anxiety and furious attack on Ann, her nurse, and other patients, which turned many against her. She refused to continue as chairperson, moved out of the room that she shared with Ann, said that she was extremely scared, and refused any attempt to try to solve the conflict.

In the team discussion next day, there was initially a dispute between Jane's nurse, who felt she had been "hysterical", and her therapist, who was very sympathetic towards her fears. In

---

*Unit meetings attended by patients, nursing staff, and consultant in which issues pertinent to the life in the community and to individuals' treatment are explored.

the discussion we thought that the nurse got caught up in siding with Ann against Jane and that this linked in with Jane's expectation of everyone being either fully on her side or completely against her. Afterwards, the nurse approached Jane saying that she probably hadn't taken her anxiety seriously enough the day before; Jane responded aggressively and contemptuously.

In her session that day, Jane said that she called Ann a psychopath, and everyone was now against her, except for Peter; she couldn't do without him. She felt scared and unsafe and wanted to go home. She talked angrily about the nurse suggesting that she was violent by harming herself—she had a right to harm herself! When the therapist pointed out that she might feel she had overreacted, she angrily said, no—she had every reason to be afraid of Ann. She hinted at frightening memories and turned away from her therapist. The therapist talked sympathetically of Jane's feeling that everyone was against her, and the patient calmed down. However, when the therapist pointed out that in Jane's mind all aggression seemed to be in Ann, whereas she had used a kind of "verbal knife" by calling Ann a "psychopath", Jane reacted aggressively: "That's nonsense! Cassel nonsense!" The therapist didn't dare to challenge her any further. Jane cried and said she was never allowed to be angry, to which the therapist responded sympathetically. Near the end of the session, Jane said that the only reason for her to stay at the Cassel was to talk to her therapist.

One can see in this session how the therapist was being pushed into being soft and completely on the patient's side, confirming Jane's views about Ann and her nurse. Whenever the therapist tried to challenge this, she was vigorously put back in her place. This seemed to be the same place that her father and Peter occupy. The other people around Jane were seen as aggressive and persecutory, but were also manipulated into being aggressive towards her and, like her nurse, were not allowed to be more sympathetic. They seemed to take the place that mother occupies in Jane's mind.

Thus, a world is created in Jane's mind in which there is a split couple of a violent, rejecting object (mother) and an ideal, loving object (father) and in which all violence is in others and none in her. This internal reality does not necessarily reflect the actual reality of the parents of her childhood, even though it may contain some truth; instead, I think, it is the result of a severe splitting process in which all hatred and violence is lodged in her internal mother and all love and care in her internal father. In the treatment setting, this scenario did not remain on the level of phantasy. The patient exerted pressure on staff and patients to actualize these split internal objects, so that nurse and therapist got into a battle with each other and Peter became the saviour of Jane from a violent, rejecting community.

Nurse and therapist were helped to see how they were enacting Jane's split internal objects and were thus enabled to approach her differently. We also addressed the conflict between Jane and Ann within the unit's patient group by taking it as a problem of the whole group: the group as a whole needed to find a solution for the "firm" chair job that Jane had stood down from. The way other patients withdrew into silence while Jane and Ann were fighting a battle also suggested that the fighting couple tallied with some dynamic in the whole group. We addressed this and were gradually able to establish an atmosphere in which other patients joined in and Jane could eventually listen to their comments. One of the other patients agreed to stand in for her for a day or two, and she promised to take the job up again after that. When she did that, she was in fact able to work with Ann more constructively than before. Interestingly, material then emerged in her therapy that put a different light on her father, of rows between her parents and of aggression from him towards Jane, as well as on her mother whom she was going to visit in hospital.

This scenario of a deeply split couple had in itself an important function for this patient: it protected her from a much more frightening scenario that came up in her initial terror when she experienced Ann and her nurse united against her—that is, of a couple united against her to throw her out or kill her. It was linked with the idea of her parents aborting her. Splitting the oedipal couple, therefore, protected her from this catastrophe. In her Russian roulette she took this catastrophe into her own hands in a perverse and omnipotent way.

More generally, this material shows how the internal objects of a patient are projected onto the external reality of other people in the hospital and how pressure can be put on them to correspond to the patient's internal reality. Such processes happen a lot in an inpatient setting and, if they remain unrecognized, confirm the patient's internal splits. If they are recognized, they need to be brought together in staff's minds in order for therapeutic work to be done on different levels: interpretatively within the transference arena of the psychotherapy, more directly in the work of the nurses, and through confrontation and interpretation of collusive group processes within the whole group. Thus the patient can be enabled to introject a more integrated version of him/herself or, indeed, a more benignly connected, thinking couple.

The meeting of individual
and group issues in everyday tasks

The reality of the Cassel setting, with the mutual interdependence of patients and staff, is very complex. Individual and group, patient, and staff dynamics become intertwined in an often complicated way that may make it difficult to know where the origin of a problem lies. It often needs enquiring into different levels of the hospital to understand the nature of the problem. I would like to illustrate this with a further example.

> Recently there was a problem around the ordering of milk. Milk for adults and adolescents needs to be ordered by the servery manager and for the families by a patient of the Families Unit; both orders go to the pantry work group, who order the milk from the hospital kitchen staff. There is an allowance of half a pint of milk for every patient, but the order was consistently higher than this allowance. In looking into this, first of all a number of individual problems emerged.

"Deirdre", an Adult Unit patient and the servery manager, ordered more milk than was allowed for the adults and adolescents. She couldn't resist the pressure from other patients to order as much as they wanted, and she also jumped if the Families Unit patient didn't do her order. Throughout her childhood, Deirdre had needed to look after her mother and provide for her while she was being abused by her father. As an adult, she was always impelled to give to others and behave as if everything was fine, even when she was very distressed or suicidal, and, as a nurse, she had turned this into her profession.

"Sandra", the patient responsible for ordering milk for the families, had recently lost her husband and was at the Cassel with her little son. She had great difficulties keeping her child's needs in mind, leading her at times to neglect him, at others to be abusive towards him. She behaved similarly in relation to the needs of the other children and parents, but for a while this was covered up by "Deirdre" stepping in.

"Helen", the pantry manager, an adolescent patient, whose responsibility it was to check the orders and pass them on to the kitchen, did so without challenging the patients who had given her the orders. The male nurse initially went along with this and seemed to be pulled into an overprotective role, which was probably linked to what she had longed for from her father who lived away from the family and left completely when she was 8 years old. When eventually the nurse challenged her, Helen became angry with him, initially refusing to do the order (which would have meant no milk for everyone), feeling unable to negotiate with the other patients involved.

Another individual reason for the increased use of milk was the excessive drinking of milk by "Claire", a patient with an eating disorder, who had hardly any other food and hadn't negotiated anything about this massive use of milk.

Thus, a whole variety of individual problems and specific pathologies turned out to be contributing to the increase in milk orders. This led to these individuals being worked with in specific ways in the community by the nurses. However, it was also felt

that there must be issues involved that concerned the wider patients' dynamic. This was particularly evident when the fridge was
being broken into and milk stolen in the night and patients tried to
cover this up. On enquiring into this, staff wondered whether the
whole scenario was an enactment of a sense of deprivation in the
patients and of a feeling in them that they were not being fed
sufficiently on an emotional level. This may have reflected the
unrealistic demand in patients for the hospital to be a rich "breast"
that can and must provide whatever they ask for, and these aspects
were addressed in different ways within the community.

The situation, however, could also be understood as a communication about the patients' perception of the actual current state of
the hospital: we were in a period where senior staff were preoccupied with their difficult relationship to a new provider, the lead
nurse was on long-term sick leave, and there were gaps and absences in the nurse group for which the others had to make up.
Thus, staff themselves did not feel sufficiently provided for, and
this would have had its effect on their capacity to provide for the
patients which they, at least unconsciously, perceived.

Conclusion

This last vignette leads me finally to an enormous difficulty in
inpatient treatment which is thought about a lot at the Cassel: the
institutional dynamics and the mutual influence of patients and
staff. A weekly large-group meeting of all clinical staff has an
important function in experiencing and thinking about processes
in the staff group. This provides an opportunity to enquire into and
work on these mutual processes, which is essential for the functioning of the institution.

Treating severely disturbed, usually very destructive patients
stirs up disturbing feelings in those working closely with them and
may lead to splitting processes in the therapeutic couple, the unit
team, or the whole hospital staff. Conflicts within the staff group
may therefore reflect problems of the patients. In addition, the
great demands put on patients in the Cassel setting provoke strong
hatred, anxiety, and resistance in patients, which staff need to deal

with. Handing a lot of responsibility to patients means that staff have to contain powerful anxieties in themselves. The conflicts around this may easily be projected into the role gap between therapists and nurses, leading to a picture of rigidly demanding nurses and softly empathic therapists. For the institution to regain its therapeutic functioning, it is important that such mutual projections are recognized and that the conflict over what can be expected of patients is turned again into a joint one.

There is, however, also the influence in the opposite direction, as the example of the milk suggests. Problems in the patient group may thus reflect conflicts in staff. Difficulties and conflicts in the senior staff or the staff group as a whole, particularly if they cannot be spoken about openly, may be projected into the patients, leading to increased acting-out and destructiveness or other such enactments. In the current health-care culture, there is also often an increased, sometimes quite destructive, pressure on the institution from outside, which leads to anxiety and tension in staff. The helplessness and anxiety of staff may then be projected into the patients, and an attempt is made to work on them there—at the wrong place.

These institutional processes, which everyone both contributes to and is pulled into, are to some degree unavoidable. Whatever form they take, they have a significant bearing on the treatment of the patients. To be able to recognize and work on these processes requires not just the capacity and willingness in staff, but reflective spaces within the institution that need to be protected. This is part of the quality of a "therapeutic institution" (Main, 1946) and a "culture of enquiry" (Main, 1983).

CHAPTER FOUR

Reflective space and group processes

Agata Pisula

E arlier in this monograph, in chapter two, Griffiths and Hinshelwood emphasize the need for reflective space to be maintained in the face of defensive attempts to avoid it by both patients and staff. They also describe how specific structures have been built into the life of the Cassel Hospital in which reasons for success and failure in everyday situations are explored in order to sustain this culture of enquiry. In this chapter, I wish to use an example of one such structure—the parents' meeting—to look more specifically at different ways the space for enquiry is maintained and the obstacles faced by both staff and patients in this joint endeavour.

As part of the treatment programme for parents who are inpatients in the Families Unit of the hospital, they attend a weekly parents' meeting (D. Flynn, 1986, 1999; Kennedy, 1986). Families admitted to the Cassel have usually broken down to such an extent that their treatment will determine whether their children will remain with them, or whether they need alternative care arrangements. The aim of this structure is to allow parents a thinking space for exploration of issues concerned with their children, who may or may not be living with them in the community, and to discuss how they might support each other. This meeting is facilitated by the principal child psychotherapist, in partnership with the senior nurse on the Families Unit. The group membership varies depending on the number of patients on the Families Unit at the time, and some patients choose not to attend.

As a qualified primary nurse working at the hospital, I was also undertaking the Cassel training in psychosocial nursing. As part of this training, I attended this meeting for a period of six weeks. This coincided with a period of absence from the meeting of the senior nurse, which meant that the group facilitator and myself were the only staff members present consistently.

My understanding of the nurse's role in this group was that she or he brought to the meeting observations and knowledge of patients from the shared everyday interactions in the life of the community; the child psychotherapist addressed more directly issues of group dynamics and child development. However, because of the wider dynamics that I discuss here, I was never able to take up this role. Also, it could be questioned whether it was realistically feasible or appropriate to achieve this in a six-week period.

My perspective remained that of a "newcomer" to the meeting. This did enable me to observe what went on in the group, as if from the outside, but it also reflected the painful confusion I sometimes felt in the face of the complexity of the processes taking place, as well as my struggle with the role of observer that I found myself in, and which I never quite managed to shake off.

The parents' meeting as an open system

To explore the complex interplay of person and setting in the parents' meeting, I will draw upon a theory of the psychology of social systems which embraces the individual, the group, and the institution (Mosse, 1994; Reed & Palmer, 1972). This frame of reference strives to integrate systems thinking with insights gained from psychoanalysis, especially Bion's work on groups (Bion, 1961; Pines, 1992) and Kleinian theory as applied to groups and institutions (Halton, 1994; Hinshelwood, 1987; Mosse, 1994).

One of the main foundations for the theory is that all living systems, and in particular social systems, require to be looked upon as open systems (Reed & Palmer, 1972). An "open system" refers to one that is open to exchange with its environment and depends upon these for its survival and development. Within this framework a group is defined as "collections or associations of people which function as systems, that is, which show signs of coordinated activity. The coordination may be consciously organised, or may take the form of spontaneous or unconscious linking between members" (Reed & Palmer, 1972, p. 1). A group defined in this way has some sort of boundary, an internal world and an external world, and depends for its activity on the regulation of its interchange with its environment. It must also have a primary task—that is, a task that the group must carry out to survive (Zagier Roberts, 1994).

Groups have not only an observable structure and functions, but also an unconscious life comparable to that described by psychoanalysis in an individual. As a result, they pursue unconscious tasks alongside the consciously identified primary task (Mosse, 1994; Reed & Palmer, 1972). The main tenet of this model is that the social and psychoanalytic perspectives must be deployed together if the life and the function of the group are to be truly understood. Thus, the impact of individual experience is made visible in the collective life and work of the group. It also allows for the investigation of how different levels of systems—from the individual to the whole organization—interpenetrate and how dynamics of one level can affect and be involved at the other level.

At the heart of this approach, attention is paid to the emotional experience of participants. Armstrong (1991) suggests that emotional experience is very rarely located within a purely individual space. He is concerned with organizations, but this perspective is of equal relevance to a group setting. The individual experience of a person-in-role in a system can be seen as an aspect of, or a facet of, the emotional experience that is contained within the inner psychic space of the organization and the interactions of its members—that is, what he terms the "space between".

The primary task of the parents' meeting, as defined by staff leading the group, is to allow patients a reflective space for exploration of issues concerned with their children. The group is firmly embedded in the context of the Families Unit, the hospital community, and the wider environment and clearly depends for its survival on its exchanges with the outside world. This is reflected in the membership of the group, which is affected by external factors like admissions and discharges, the material that patients bring to the meeting which is taken from their day-to-day life in the hospital, and the very setting itself which is in a room next to the patients' common-room.

In order to survive and develop as a system, a group requires the exercise of a regulatory function, controlling its exchanges with its environment. In the case of a working group, these include meeting physical necessities, accepting, selecting, or rejecting new members, and controlling exchanges of information. By the decisions it makes about such transactions, the group determines the nature of its boundaries and therefore its own character. Regulation of the boundary transactions of a group is a function that may at different times be performed by different members (Reed & Palmer, 1972).

The membership of the parents' group is open to all patients on the Families Unit, but it is voluntary. Patients exercise boundary control by choosing whether to attend and, in fact, two patients regularly absented themselves during the time I attended the group. Also, on one occasion, an absent patient was fetched by others who felt that it was important for her to come to the meeting and talk about the difficulties she had in caring for her son.

To a large extent, patients also determined the content of the discussions, as the material brought to the group, and the individuals who chose to speak, tended to be self-selected. However, the majority of the patients chose to remain silent in the meetings, and, as we shall discuss later, the meaning of this silence remained unexplored.

Within the open-systems framework, the fundamental aspect of leadership is boundary control, which includes being clear about the primary task, attending to the flow of information across the boundary, and ensuring that the group has the resources it needs (Zagier Roberts, 1994). The facilitator clearly performed such a function for the group. This was illustrated by the first parents' meeting I attended. The facilitator and myself were the first people in the room. He indicated that I should sit opposite him rather than next to him. After some time, patients started drifting in. Eventually, after asking about the whereabouts of a couple of missing patients, he started the meeting. He acknowledged the presence of a new patient and asked for someone to explain the task of the meeting to her. He also indicated who should not do it, as one of the patients often took that role upon herself. Another patient then explained the purpose of the meeting as a place where parents could bring issues about their children. She also questioned the need for patients without children in the hospital, like herself, to be there. The facilitator responded to this by pointing out that problems raised in the meeting might touch on the personal experiences of everybody.

Thus, the facilitator looked after the time boundaries, clarified the task of the meeting, and influenced the seating arrangements and the flow of communication in the group. It was also apparent that it was he who decided when it was appropriate to move things on in the meeting and who set limits on what was appropriate for the group to discuss or on what language was considered acceptable.

It was very noticeable that when the facilitator was absent, the patient group took a much more active role in both boundary control and boundary testing. At one of the meetings, he was absent and a senior nurse was present in his place. The meeting started even later than usual, and a considerable number of patients were absent. After a long silence, I asked whether there was anything patients wanted to discuss. This provoked an immediate response from two of the patients, who became involved in a very heated argument, which appeared to be a continuation of a long-standing conflict. The senior nurse who was in the role of group facilitator commented that the discussion was more appropriate to a different forum, but this went unheeded. A number of patients expressed a wish that "something should be done about it", as if expecting the two nurses present in the room—myself being one of them—to step in and deal with the situation. This kind of response from the patients was more like those seen in "firm" meetings. On the whole, nurses take a much more active and confrontative role in these meetings and it seemed that patients were expecting us to take up this same role in the parents' meeting. Eventually, it was a strong verbal expression of frustration and impatience from one of the patients, and her comment that "children are being forgotten", that allowed the meeting to move on and do some work.

This example brings up not only boundary issues but also the issue of group identity. In order to survive and develop, a group not only has to regulate its exchange with its environment, it also has to preserve among its members a sense of its own identity. This means protecting its members shared internal model of the group from too radical or rapid changes (Reed & Palmer, 1972).

What it indicated was that the parents' group was held together by the facilitator, who was like the hub of the group, with the other members like spokes in a wheel, and that the group's identity was dependent on his presence. I was reminded of that quite emphatically when I was encouraging a patient to attend the group on a day that he was absent. She responded: "Oh, but he won't be there", as if he literally were the group. His absence drastically affected the structure of the group, causing considerable disturbance and change in the mode of functioning.

Unconscious life of the parents' meeting

The examples given so far already hint at two levels that coexist in the life of the group: enacted, non-verbal channels of communication occurring alongside the verbal life of the group, and pursuit of unconscious tasks alongside the stated ones (Hinshelwood, 1987; Mosse, 1994; Reed & Palmer, 1972; Zagier Roberts, 1994).

The individual's own unconscious internal world impinges on the interpersonal relations in the group. Psychoanalysis of the individual has recognized certain kinds of "primitive" phantasies at the root of human personality that give rise to unrealistic terrors, anxieties, and guilt. But even though they may appear unrealistic to an outsider, to the individual concerned they have a compelling reality derived from the experience of his or her internal world of "objects". The more disturbed the individual, the more she or he experiences her or his internal world to be fraught and threatened.

Related to these phantasies, and the intolerable feelings they give rise to, are the unconscious defence mechanisms of projection, introjection, identification, and splitting. In a group situation, they become collective defences organized within the culture of the group. From this viewpoint, group boundary problems can be seen as collective expressions of individual members' internal emotional states derived from the operation of these primitive defence mechanisms.

In the example described earlier of a meeting from which the facilitator was absent, the physical withdrawal of the group members, as well as the argument that dominated a large part of the meeting, could be understood as a defensive measure adopted by patients in the face of a perceived threat to the group identity. Hinshelwood (1987) points out that fear of annihilation by fragmentation is central to the life of a community of patients with disturbed personalities and that membership of such groups brings a particular susceptibility to "annihilation by forces within".

Any manifestation of fragility within the structure of a group or community arouses deep-seated anxieties in its individual members about "going to pieces" themselves and their lack of integration. Considerable effort is then employed in collectively fending off this threat of fragmentation. The collective nature of the defences employed is an important characteristic, as it provides cohesiveness and allows the group to operate as a whole. In this particular meeting, two individuals got locked into a confrontation that seemed to have no resolution while others took the opportunity to be comfortable onlookers whose only function was to keep the two in their roles.

Hinshelwood (1987) describes the process that takes place within a group through which an intervention can lead to two alternative outcomes. The first is conscious verbalization of an emotional state (a true therapeutic aim), the second an enacted display of the internal object relations which get acted out in an unconscious drama in the group. Rather than verbal expression of feelings and phantasies, an active manipulation of self and others into roles takes place. Hinshelwood calls this "dramatization". The way in which people in groups place each other in roles corresponds to the unconscious positioning of "objects" in individual psychoanalysis, and the intrusion of emotional dramatizations into group situations corresponds to the notion of transference. Dramatization is a manifestation of transference at the group level.

Conscious verbalization was evident in one meeting when a mother brought up an incident between her 3-year-old son and an 8-year-old boy whose mother was also present in the meeting. The older boy apparently threatened the younger one by saying: "My grandad has a gun and will blow your brains out." The conversation quickly turned to the issue of whether there was a real gun that the boy had seen and whether it was negligent of his mother to allow this to happen. A number of patients joined in, describing the boy as very aggressive and uncontrollable and saying that his mother was ineffectual in her dealings with him. She responded by defending her efforts to discipline him. I began to feel rather uncomfortable, as the atmosphere became charged and hostile. The facilitator attempted to intervene but was interrupted. Eventually he whistled and said: "I am the referee here", which elicited laughter and defused tension. The atmosphere changed quite dramatically, and patients became calmer and spoke in a more reflective way. The facilitator returned to the original issue and helped the patients to formulate the problem as: "How do you respond when an older child says inappropriate things to a younger one?" Later in the meeting, he also made a connection between the phrase used by the boy, "blow your brains out", and how his mother got blown to pieces in her mind by her child's behaviour, an interpretation that she was able to accept.

The splitting off and projection of either aggression or incompetence into another group member seemed quite a common pattern in this group. The process, started off by one patient but quickly supported by others, created a scapegoat—the 8-year-old's mother—who ended up holding all the unwanted parts of the group. This situation was re-enacted over a number of meetings as this mother came to represent some sort of "sponge" for the group's unwanted feelings of failure and incompetence. This process allowed other patients some relief from the guilt that is normally associated with feelings of this kind if owned. It also indicated that this mother identified to some extent with the role assigned to her, as evidenced in the way she provoked the repetition by eagerly raising issues about her children in almost every meeting that I was present in. On other occasions, the unwanted feelings got projected outside the group. Often these were projected into the patients on the Adult Unit in the hospital, who were then experienced as collectively unhelpful and uncaring and were exposing the children to irresponsible behaviour by their outbursts of uncontrollable anger.

The facilitator's awareness of these group dynamics enabled him to intervene at a critical point. He used humour in an effective way, creating a palpable change of atmosphere in the meeting. The dynamics of the group were not explicitly acknowledged by him; rather, the emphasis was on the clarification and interpretation of the individual problem. The verbal interaction that followed allowed the patients to return to the primary task of the group and think through some of the issues involved. A connection was also made between the child's behaviour and the mother's fragmented state of mind, which she was able to accept in the less hostile atmosphere at the end of the meeting, in contrast to the earlier criticisms which just led to dramatization. There was a feeling of energy and connectedness between the group members at the end of this particular meeting which I think reflected the release of creative capacity in the patients which then got channelled into thinking about the problem.

The process of "dramatization" (Hinshelwood, 1987) was also evident. Just before one meeting, it suddenly became apparent that, due to a failure of communication, there were going to be four members of staff present in the group. A fractious few minutes followed prior to the meeting, during which I felt that the facilitator was dismissing everything I said. I felt particularly humiliated as I recounted an incident in which a mother had used the phrase "wanking off" in talking to her older son. I said that I considered her use of language inappropriate, while he commented that this was the use of the vernacular. I went into the meeting feeling upset, and I remained silent throughout. During the meeting, the facilitator objected to the use of the phrase "the little sod" used by a mother to describe one of the children. This woman was my patient. A heated exchange followed between them, the patient defending her use of the phrase and the facilitator insisting that it was inappropriate. The argument remained unresolved and eventually he moved the meeting on. After the group, the staff present got into a further argument about how it came about that all four of us were present. It seemed that the staff fragmentation and conflict had spilled into the meeting. As a result, the facilitator's intervention led to some sort of re-enactment of an unresolved conflict, with no resolution available. My patient may also have sensed my unexpressed anger towards the facilitator, which she ended up enacting for me. It is also possible that a sudden influx of staff into the meeting who were much more vocal than myself undermined the central position that the facilitator normally held in the meeting. The patient might have ended up expressing something on behalf of either the staff group or the whole group in her challenge to his authority.

The nature of group activity in the parents' meeting

The examples given so far illustrate another pattern that appeared to be typical in this group: an oscillation between defensive activity and work activity. Reed and Palmer (1972) point to two main theories of group behaviour. The first is a model of the developmental phases of groups to a state in which certain distinctive qualities of relationships and work may be observed (Wright, 1989). The second theoretical perspective identifies an oscillation between the work and defensive (survival) activity, with no assumption that the group progresses from one to the other (Bion, 1961). Bion argues that a small group can exist in two states: as a sophisticated workgroup and as what he called a basic assumption group, which can be understood as defensive or regressive manifestations of group life. This model is more useful in understanding groups in which internal relationships are continually being affected by external influences and those with a long life-span, both of which were the case for the parents' meeting described above.

In Bion's formulation, a group has to struggle continuously in the maintenance of the conscious and explicit task of the group in the teeth of being dragged back into primitive group behaviour dominated by basic assumption mentality. Turquet (1985) describes some of the characteristics of the workgroup as its desire to know and acquire insight, to discover and understand explanations, concern with the consequences of its own behaviour and action, and collective responsibility for the group's interactions, both internally between members and externally in the interchange with the environment.

At times, the parents' meeting certainly exhibited some or all of these characteristics. Patients' active involvement with each other, the support and understanding offered, could be very impressive, while the search for understanding rather than expectation of staff intervention common to firm meetings was carefully fostered by the facilitator.

At other times, the group behaviour clearly exhibited elements of basic assumption activity. Groups caught up in basic assumption mentality divert into a maladaptive culture that shows a tendency towards avoidance of the primary task; the group's behaviour is instead directed at attempting to meet the unconscious needs of its members by reducing anxiety and internal conflicts. Bion describes three group cultures, each suffused with an unspoken basic assumption. In basic assumption dependency, the group behaves as if its primary task is solely to provide for the satisfaction of the needs and wishes of its members and becomes pathologically dependent on its leader. In basic assumption fight–flight, the group has an enemy to be either attached to or fled from. Basic assumption pairing is based on the collective and unconscious belief that a pairing between two members within the group, or perhaps between the leader of the group and some external person, will solve all the actual problems and needs of the group.

In the meeting from which the facilitator was absent, the absenteeism and a fight between two patients, which effectively stopped the group from pursuing its primary task, could be seen as an expression of basic assumption fight–flight in response to a perceived threat to the identity of the meeting.

Bion (1961) also refers to what he terms the sophisticated use of basic assumption mentality. He suggests that a group may utilize it in a sophisticated way, by mobilizing the emotions of one basic assumption in the constructive pursuit of the primary task. It may have been that the dependency on the facilitator, so clearly exhibited in the examples already given, represented a sophisticated use of basic assumption dependency, as it encouraged the patients in their search for understanding. Similarly, Stokes (1994) suggests that different professions adopt different sophisticated uses of basic assumption mentality and that the training of therapists tends to idealize the pairing between therapist and client as a pre-eminent medium for change. This might explain the predominance of individual interpretations offered by the facilitator, to the detriment of group ones. This might also have contributed to the structuring of communications within the group, which often consisted of a few patients who actively engaged in interchanges with him while the rest remained silent.

Types of interactions

The majority of interventions in the parents' meeting were verbal, and I have already given examples of some of these and of the different effects that they might have had on the group. On the whole, the facilitator tended to ask for clarification or offer interpretation while the patient members of the group offered advice or shared their own experiences of parenting. Humour was used at times by the facilitator in an effective way to either diffuse tension or illustrate a point that he was making in a more graphic way. Occasionally, a non-verbal intervention was engaged in in a very concrete way—for instance, when the facilitator offered a tissue to a crying patient or when patients fetched a missing member of the group. One crucial non-verbal intervention was the use of silence. The facilitator would often remain silent for periods of time, letting the group take its course. When offered, a comment was on the whole less directive and less confrontative than is the case in "firm" meetings, previously described. This attitude enabled interactions between patients to develop and fostered their involvement in the group.

Roles

I would like to turn now to the roles, both conscious and unconscious, that members of the group took up. Reed and Palmer (1972) define a small group as one in which every member can form a distinct impression of every other member. The participant has some picture of each member, or a feeling towards him or her. The model of the group that forms in the mind of the group member includes an image of each individual member. Through this process, a small group builds up a pattern of mutually accepted roles, which provide each person with a sense of belonging to the group and of having a distinctive part in it. This process occurs on both conscious and unconscious levels.

On the conscious level, the group is formally divided into facilitator and group members. However, the unconscious roles taken up by different individuals are much more varied. It has already been described how individuals find themselves assigned unconscious roles through the process of dramatization.

Hinshelwood (1987) outlines a complex relationship between an individual and the group. On the one hand, the individual externalizes his or her own internal object-relations as dramatizations in the group, but, on the other, individuals become engaged in dramatized roles when they have some specific adaptability or "valency" for the roles needed. Roles assigned in the dramatized relationships are varied and changeable. Different individuals are brought into play as they become, in turn, the people most suited to play out the required attitudes and relationships of the moment. The facilitator would often be perceived as an "expert," with the rest of the group looking up to him for answers. One patient would often either end up in a fight with someone or alternatively perform the role of the "joker", using humour in a very defensive way. Another patient usually took up the role of the "wise owl" of the group. She was often able to give good advice to other patients but hardly ever exposed her own vulnerabilities. As was described earlier, one of the patients was persistently assigned a role of a scapegoat. This is a very common process that allows other group members to avoid issues of responsibility, blame, and guilt.

Hinshelwood (1987) suggests that what he calls "an unchanging individual" holds a particular place in an organization where individuals are expected to change themselves. Patients can avoid feeling criticized for their lack of activity by directing hostility towards one individual who is occupying the attention of the meeting. Critical attention then focuses on this "unchanging individual" who is pushed towards the centre of the stage as the person standing against the help offered. In this way, the scapegoated individual carries all the criticism and blame for the waste of the opportunities, the "sin", that really belongs to the whole group.

All the roles mentioned so far were the ones taken up by patients who consistently contributed to the meetings. The silence of a large part of the group went, on the whole, unacknowledged, and therefore the role played by this silent majority can only be speculated about. It was a form of communication that could be understood on a number of levels.

Griffiths and Hinshelwood (1997) point out that when patients are faced with stresses of community life "it is impressive how much their previous symptomatology by which they expressed themselves fades away, to be substituted by a hostile vocal (or silent) protest at the hospital and staff. In such a protest they often find the beginnings of real colleagueship . . ." (p. 6). Certainly, a group culture consisting of sullen and unresponsive patients passively resisting tyrannical criticism by staff (real or imaginary) reflects the common dynamics of many of the meetings in the hospital community. However, Hinshelwood (1987) also suggests that patients' despair may not be recognized often enough, while anger is overemphasized, and that a member of staff can easily feel attacked when the patient is actually trying to convey despair. It might be that fear of releasing explosive hostility or overwhelming despair were some of the reasons that the silence remained unexplored, especially at a time when the staff group was not feeling very robust.

Finally, Hinshelwood (1987) suggests that the silent member of a group seems to abolish the boundary between the individual and group, allowing for a bizarre merged relationship with the group. These are often the patients who are functioning on the most primitive undifferentiated level with very poor ability to judge the reality of the life of the group and limited capacity for working in the interpersonal arena.

In relation to my own role in these meetings, I think that it is already clear from this account how much I took on the role of a silent observer. This role was assigned to me formally by the facilitator, who indicated from early on that I would not be able to learn in six weeks the way of working in a group which had developed over years. The facilitator had been unhappy about the absence of the senior nurse in the meeting, and perhaps unhappy that the resulting staff pairing was with a nurse "in training" rather than a senior nurse on the Families Unit. However valid these comments might have been, they had the effect of silencing me almost completely. I felt that skills gained in "firm" and community meetings were seen as inappropriate for the parents' meeting, and I felt very deskilled.

A conflict developed between us that was largely unacknowledged by either of us. It was partly to do with my struggles with a role that had been imposed on me and did not fit particularly well. Some of it, I felt, belonged to the wider dynamics of the hospital: issues of authority and power that had been very alive in the community over the previous few months; the perceived threat to analytic thinking space within the hospital culture; and the struggle to allow space for concerns about children. It seems that somehow I came to represent some of these issues.

In part, this conflict might also have been a reflection of an ongoing tension between clinical and learning needs that nurses confront throughout their Cassel training in psychosocial nursing. The structuring of the course means that they are full-time employees of the hospital with clinical responsibilities and are part of the nursing establishment, while at the same time they have trainee status. The decision for "course" nurses to attend the parents' meeting was made during the review of training and was guided by learning needs. However, the rotation of nurses on a six-weekly basis had a major effect on the continuity of the group and could be seen as anti-therapeutic from a clinical point of view. Also, there was no clarification of the learning objectives for the nurses-in-training attending the parents' meeting, and of the fact that realistically the role of an observer in the parents' meeting was appropriate for such a short period of time.

My own contribution to the problem was my inability to step out of the assigned role in the meeting. I was able to raise issues with the facilitator outside the group but remained more or less silent throughout the six weeks in the group. On reflection, this was due to my difficulty in trusting my own emotional experience and risking public exposure. I did not feel safe enough to allow myself to make mistakes. As I have already indicated, the only time I was able to take a fairly active part and offer some of my experiences to the group was in the meeting in which the facilitator was absent.

Conclusion

A number of authors (Denford & Griffiths, 1993; Gabbard, 1992; Janssen, 1993, 1994) point out that, in contrast to individual therapy, in psychoanalytically informed hospital treatment the transference–countertransference relationships are dispersed amongst a multiplicity of relationships and the patients develop multiple transferences to the staff and to the institution which need to be processed systematically if the value of the therapeutic milieu is to be fully realized.

Furthermore, Hinshelwood (1987) describes how the primitive levels of anxiety that patients operate on leads them to perceive the community as the only thing that can save them from the terrors of their internal world. As a result, the staff group are continuously scrutinized for their ability or potential failure to maintain the community's function as this relieving container. The phantasies developed about staff as transference objects lead to very complex unspoken attitudes. If they remain unverbalized, they can only be expressed in dramatized form. However, even though comparisons between members of staff and observation of their personalities and interrelationships provide one of the major preoccupations and anxieties in the community, they are hardly ever expressed openly. The danger is that the more these issues go unspoken, the more they feel unspeakable and increasingly play into patients' internal conflicts and contradictions and support the fear that in-tense emotional experiences are unresolvable and insoluble.

Hinshelwood (1987) points out that these conflict situations amongst staff present an extremely important therapeutic value if the reality of them can be explicitly acknowledged and verbalized. However, the example of the parents' meeting described in this chapter show the difficulties faced by staff in using such a situation therapeutically.

CHAPTER FIVE

Reflections
on a supervisory relationship

Pamela Pringle

I n this chapter I explore a supervisory relationship with a junior nursing colleague following my own promotion to a nursing position with managerial responsibilities. Clinical supervision at the Cassel Hospital is recognized as an important tool that supports the often very difficult work with patients. This supervisory relationship presented me with challenges that came at a point in my career when I felt that I did not possess some of the skills required to help me cope adequately. However, with help from my own supervisor I was able to understand and integrate some of the interpersonal processes that occurred within this supervisory relationship, and I went on to develop a productive working relationship with my colleague. The chapters in this monograph explore some of the difficulties in allowing ourselves to enquire into practice. By examining the nature of the relationship between my colleague and myself, I discuss some of the problems we faced in achieving this. I then go on to look at how we managed to overcome our problems using clinical supervision as a reflective space. In order to give this relationship a context, I outline some of the staff meetings in the Cassel Hospital that support enquiry and understanding, which in themselves are vital to the work that we do with patients.

Working with the patient group is not easy. They often come to us with a history of neglect and deprivation, and some are the victims of emotional, physical, and sexual abuse. Their relationships with others can be disturbed, and their feelings of anger and self-loathing can be manifested in self-mutilation and suicide attempts. Helping patients process their feelings and begin to change their ways of relating can arouse powerful feelings in staff members. Managing the anxiety generated in teams when working with such patients can lead to professional boundaries being used defensively. Staff members can resort to primitive defence mechanisms, splitting off hostile feelings and projecting them on to another person, often a different professional within the team (Gabbard, 1994; Woodhouse & Pengelly, 1991).

Tom Main, in his seminal paper "The Ailment" (1957), believed that if such feelings are not attended to the staff team can end up being frustrated, angry, and split. In recognition of this phenomena, regular meetings have been incorporated into the Cassel Hospital timetable whereby members of the multidisciplinary team can talk about their work and the feelings generated by their patients. Attempts are made to understand these feelings and use them in their work with patients. In nurse/therapist supervision, for example, senior staff can help the therapeutic pair to understand how the patient is using the nurse and therapist in conscious and unconscious ways and how this may fit into his or her previous experience (James, 1986). As well as the regular multidisciplinary meetings, there are other meetings such as nurse handovers. In these, the night nurse communicates the nights' events, including his or her own emotional experience of the shift, to the oncoming day nursing staff. There is also a weekly meeting at which nurses can share the stresses and strains of working in an intensive environment with disturbed and difficult patients. The Cassel Hospital, therefore, offers an environment in which professional anxieties can be revealed, explored, and hopefully contained, with resulting benefits for patients. Staff are enabled to carry on with the experience of the everyday work using insights gained as tools to help patients change and develop.

The nurses who work at the Cassel Hospital have a basic nursing qualification and substantial experience before they undertake the hospital-based Diploma in Psychosocial Nursing, which further equips them to work within this specialized environment. However, no matter what their level of expertise, all nurses can expect to receive individual supervision. This plays an important part in facilitating discussion and thought about practice issues. Clinical supervision is associated with psychoanalytic training and practice and has long been adopted by other professional groups, such as social workers. However, it is increasingly acknowledged as a means for helping nurses to deal with the high emotional cost associated with nursing activities (Butterworth & Faugier, 1992). The United Kingdom Central Council for Nursing, Midwifery and Health Visiting believes that clinical supervision plays a vital part in ensuring safe and effective standards of care (UKCC, 1996).

Clinical supervision

There are many methods and definitions of supervision—for example, there is clinical, managerial, and training supervision—but common to each type are the functions of management, education, and support (Kadushin, 1976; Proctor, 1986). Platt-Koch (1986) suggested that the goals of clinical supervision in nursing are to expand the knowledge base of the practitioner, to assist in developing clinical proficiency, and to develop autonomy and self-esteem as a professional. Butterworth and Faugier (1992) concur with this and add that supervision is an enabling process, which is an opportunity for personal and professional growth. Supervision takes the form of a working alliance in which practice issues can be presented and feedback and guidance given. The knowledge, skills, and attitudes of nurses are developed, which is a means of ensuring the best possible care for patients (Simms, 1993). In mental health nursing, supervision has been described as a protective mechanism for patients in that they are protected from the nurse who feels that he or she knows best (Barker, 1992). Supervision can take place on a one-to-one or group basis and can be offered by one's peers or by a colleague. There are those who believe that supervision should be arranged with a colleague who has more experience and a higher knowledge level (Wright, 1993). This sometimes may be the nurse's manager. Although the UKCC (1996) has also said that clinical supervision is not a management tool, nurses have in the past viewed the overseeing of clinical practice with some suspicion (Hill, 1989). Platt-Koch (1986) believes that supervision is neither a means of observation by an administrative superior who inspects, directs, controls, and evaluates the nurse's work, nor psychotherapy. The purpose of supervision is to help the nurse increase skill in working with the patient, whereas the purpose of psychotherapy is to help resolve inner conflicts.

The fear of being "analysed", as well as being subjected to a formalized system of accountability, may account for the reservations that some nurses have had about receiving clinical supervision. However, Kohner (1994) has suggested that it is the skill of the supervisor that is important for nurses to feel that supervision is a worthwhile endeavour. Kohner (1994) lists some of the qualities needed by nursing supervisors. These include being a teacher, a listener, a facilitator, and a confidence builder, and being supportive, flexible, objective, and a skilled practitioner. Preliminary enquiries into the experiences of clinical supervision by mental health nurses suggest that good-enough supervision is the exception rather than the rule. Nursing supervisors seem to lack the training to be able to process the supervisory relationship effectively, and thus they hold back individual nurses in their development. They are unable to provide sufficient emotional containment to enable nurses to think clearly about the emotional content of therapeutic relationships with their patients (Scanlon & Weir, 1997). As a result of their enquiries, Scanlon and Weir (1997) indicate that a skilled practitioner who is not the nurse's supervisor perhaps best offers clinical supervision. Platt-Koch (1986) argues that it is better if a supervisor has no administrative power over the supervisee, as it can be difficult for the nurse to expose vulnerabilities and imperfections. However, this is not always possible, as managers are sometimes also supervisors. A supervisor, whether or not a line manager, is placed in a position where good professional standards have to be upheld.

In this exploration here of a supervisory relationship, I aim to address the difficulties in providing a containing space for a nursing colleague for whom I had managerial responsibility. In other words, I wish to examine the inherent conflict in balancing the managerial, educative, and supportive functions of supervision. As a supervisor, I myself did not feel sufficiently skilled to tackle this challenge effectively, although I believe that I did possess some of the qualities as listed by Kohner (1994). I aim to show that, despite our difficulties, my colleague and I were able to work out a relationship within the context of clinical supervision that became mutually beneficial in terms of both of our personal and professional development.

Case study

My supervisory relationship with "Sarah" began when I got a new job as a unit senior nurse in the hospital. This role required management of the nursing resources on the unit and overseeing nursing practice. The unit had undergone a time of change, with several staff members leaving and new ones beginning. There were changes on other units too, and several nurses had applied for these senior positions, Sarah included. She had worked in the hospital for a similar length of time to myself, but despite her qualifications and experience was not appointed. Sarah remained a primary nurse on the unit I moved to. At first, our relationship was cordial. We had known each other a long time and had worked well together. We met each week for supervision, and in our meetings I aimed to consider the three functions of supervision: management, support, and education (Kadushin, 1976). These help the nurse by giving support to cope with the demands of developing and exploring practice, offering a managerial perspective to situations and experiences that the nurse encounters, and providing new information and identifying educational opportunities (Northcott, 1998).

As well as thinking about work with patients, I felt that we needed to address the issue of the recent promotions and how this might have an impact on our working relationship. It is important at this point to say that I did not keep notes of our meetings, and so my recollections have to contend with the passage of time. Nevertheless, I do remember certain events and feelings that convey a sense of the problems we faced. It felt hugely uncomfortable for me to raise the issue of my being promoted and Sarah not having got the senior nursing job she had applied for. I could not help but think that this must have a bearing on how we would work together, as I was now responsible for overseeing her nursing practice, where previously she had been a peer. Yet we could not speak openly about this fact. Sarah only spoke of her general disappointment with the institution, feeling that her work was not valued. I did not push her to say any more than this—to do so felt as if I were rubbing her nose in the fact that I had got my job while she had not. I felt guilty and as if I was being cruel to expect her to say any more about it. However, our failure to confront this change in status did not go away. I increasingly felt Sarah's resentment, initially through my interactions with one of her patients. It seemed to me that the patient took every opportunity to contradict me or challenge me in various nurse and patient meetings. There was one occasion when both Sarah and her patient, in a fashion that made me feel humiliated, challenged a decision I had made about the refurbishment of a room. On another occasion, the patient said that I did not have the best interests of the unit at heart and accused me of not looking after things properly. If I made an intervention in a group meeting, the patient would sometimes get up and walk out angrily. I became increasingly unsure of myself in any interaction I had with this particular patient, although I still felt confident in my dealings with other patients on the unit.

In our supervision meetings, Sarah became increasingly critical of my abilities as a more senior nurse. Like the patient, she pointed out my failure to look after things properly. She told me that I did not look after her well enough—for example, our supervision meetings were not happening regularly. Hawkins and Shohet (1989) state that it is important to be clear about the practical boundaries of supervision, such as the times, frequency, place, and what might be allowed to interrupt the session. I do recall that sometimes our supervision would be postponed because of pressing clinical demands. However, in retrospect, it would have been more important to protect our meeting times. I was probably avoiding Sarah because it was easier at the time to try to push away the uncomfortable truth of my lack of confidence at not having the skills to deal with a difficult situation. Sarah also told me that I did not take care of other junior nurses either. She pointed out an incident in which I had not informed them of a planned absence. In regard to her patient caseload, Sarah gave me the impression that she thought she was more of an expert than I was, although she did discuss her work with me in supervision.

The managerial function of the supervisory role calls upon the supervisor to help workers look at their work, as even the most experienced worker will have blind spots and areas of vulnerability and prejudice. As noted earlier, for many nurses this aspect of "quality control" is unwelcome and uncomfortable, yet the supervisor, whether line manager or not, is placed in a position where professional standards have to be upheld. This may imply managerial action either from the supervisor or from someone on his or her behalf. In Sarah's case, I did not need to take any managerial action in respect of her nursing care; her clinical skills were of a high quality, and I could easily get a sense of her work from my observations in various meetings. The unique setting of the therapeutic community means that work with patients is open to enquiry from one's colleagues. Both Sarah and I could rely on this factor. However, the difficulty in my relationship with Sarah effectively wiped out anything extra that I could offer her in the way of support or help. It also meant that I was not giving myself the chance to develop my own confidence and skill at helping Sarah work with her patients. This was a new aspect to my role, which I needed to learn. Hawkins and Shohet (1989) note how the supportive function of supervision is a means of responding to the way in which intimate therapeutic work with clients can affect workers. It is of primary importance that the supervisor supports the worker in forming, developing, and sustaining a therapeutic relationship with his or her patient or client. Workers necessarily open themselves to the distress, pain, and fragmentation of the client and therefore need time to become aware of how this has affected them and to deal with any reactions. Not attending to these emotions soon leads to less-than-effective workers who become either over-identified with the clients or defended against being further affected by them. This can lead to stress and burn-out (Hawkins & Shohet, 1989). There was no evidence to suggest that Sarah was burnt out, but the unspoken tension between us denied her an opportunity to explore the transference or countertransference that may have been brought up by her work with patients. Further understanding of the psychological and social functioning of one particular patient was hindered. Sarah could also have used our supervision meetings to think about her professional development; she was obviously suffering from the effects of missing out on a promotion. She herself felt that her confidence and motivation had been affected. She said that she just wanted to get on with the job she was being paid to do. Nevertheless, it was not that simple. Sarah's and my own feelings about my change in status were being played out in our supervisory relationship and also through one of her patient's frequent attacks on my capabilities.

Sarah's challenge to my authority as a new manager could be perceived as emerging from resentment at my having got what she had been denied. As Joseph (1986) explains, it is very difficult to face another's success, enjoyment, and pleasure, and the nearer to home this gets, the more difficult this is likely to feel. These feelings are uncomfortable for people to bear, and most try to protect themselves from experiencing envy with various manoeuvres. One way is to idealize the person, thus putting such feelings out of reach. One can devalue oneself, making out that one has nothing to give, again increasing the gap between oneself and the object of envy. Another way is to take up and "swallow" the other person's ideas without properly digesting them, thus rendering that person redundant, or one can stir up envious attacking feelings in other people, getting them to do the work for you. Perhaps this explains some of the patient's attacks on me. I tried to discuss this particular patient's hatred of me in a supervision session with Sarah. She said that she had no idea why this patient disliked me so much, as her relationship with the patient was fine. I did feel that there was some connection between my relationship with Sarah and the patient's relationship with me. Sarah's own personal feelings about her situation were preventing her from seeing what was happening with this patient. Another important aspect of this scenario is that patients with a borderline personality disorder in particular can often detect latent qualities within clinicians that serve as a convenient hook for projected aspects of the patient (Gabbard, 1994). It was possible that this patient had found convenient targets in both Sarah and myself. I became the person who could never do anything right, while Sarah was a "good object". It was important for all our sakes to resolve the conscious and unconscious conflict between us. In this way, supervision could become a useful working tool for Sarah, for myself, and for her patient. The patient could be helped to integrate the good and bad aspects of both of us and herself—an important part of treatment.

How, then, did we emerge from this situation? As a supervisor, I felt undermined and deskilled in my dealings with Sarah; our once amicable relationship was under a certain amount of strain. Brown and Bourne (1996) note how internal promotion is a common event that often causes pain and ill-feeling. They say that major adjustments in role relationships are needed to avoid some of the tensions evoked when a former peer becomes the boss. They suggest that there needs to be a very open exchange between supervisor and supervisee at the outset in order to think through the steps needed to manage the new situation. They acknowledge the difficulties in this and suggest moving to another team or bringing in an external consultant if the situation cannot be resolved.

In my own and Sarah's situation, attempts at exploring the new relationship for both of us met with little success. However, my own clinical supervisor was a helpful third party to both Sarah and myself. I was able to think through strategies that could help move our relationship forward. The way forward proved to be through Sarah's position as the most experienced nurse on the unit at that time. This meant that she was expected to stand in for me during my absence. Her responsibilities included making decisions about patients as a more senior member of the multidisciplinary team. She also needed to manage the nursing resources on the unit. My role was to help Sarah prepare for more managerial-type responsibilities, not only for the smooth running of the unit but also in terms of her continuing professional development. Thought needed to be given to how she could begin to prepare herself for promotion in the future. I was encouraged in this course of action by my own manager, and without her encouragement to be persistent I would have found the process even more difficult. Sarah let me know that she felt unwilling to take on an extended role, as she had so recently been rejected for a managerial position; however, her thoughts gradually changed.

Winnicott (1986) observed that using constructive activity is a way of getting people to see their destructiveness. At the same time as becoming more aware of destructiveness, constructive activity is made possible. Giving Sarah an opportunity to use her creativity, through taking on an extended role, began to help her work through her feeling of resentment. Winnicott (1986) suggests that when a sense of guilt about destructive activity becomes conscious, then constructive activity can result. It is difficult for people to take responsibility for their own destructiveness, but when they can they do not need to use the technique of projection in order to cope with their own destructive impulses and thoughts in such a powerful way. This approach does have risks attached. Providing creative opportunities does not always work. The opportunities may be falsely used and are eventually withdrawn because they are felt to be false. Also, if opportunity is offered to someone who is unable to get to the destructiveness, it is felt as a reproach. In Sarah's case, she began to accept her personal destructive urges, and, from this, constructive activity could begin. The catalyst for change was the intervention of a third party.

Sarah felt a sense of guilt about our deteriorating relationship; this developed while I was on leave. My own supervisor had met up with Sarah, as a supportive measure, helping her with her nursing managerial responsibilities during my absence. Sarah had agreed to take on this role as the most experienced nurse on the unit, despite her initial reservations. My supervisor had used this opportunity to get her to think over recent events and her attitude towards me. When I returned from my holiday, Sarah told me that she had been grateful for the directness of this approach. We began to talk about the difficulty on both our parts in confronting the change in our relationship. Sarah said it was easy for her to sit back and be critical of me, without having to hold managerial responsibility. The reality of having to do this in my absence helped her change her attitude. Sarah was ready now to think further about the extra responsibilities that she would like to take on to help her prepare for future promotion. In regard to Sarah's patient, I continued to have an uncomfortable relationship with her, but I no longer felt as persecuted by her. Although she remained critical on occasions, our relationship felt calmer. Sarah developed into a respected and trusted colleague whom I missed greatly when she eventually left the hospital to take up a senior nursing position elsewhere.

Conclusion

At the heart of clinical supervision must be the patient, with both supervisor and supervisee concentrating on improvements in patient care and nursing practice. In this case study, I have shown that a personal and professional relationship can stand in the way of examining patient issues effectively. Clinical supervision may be easier if it is offered by a skilled and experienced practitioner who is not the nurse's line manager, but for some nurses this is not possible. The powerful feelings that can emerge during the course of a professional relationship within the bounds of clinical supervision need to be understood and worked through if supervision sessions are to be made a good-enough environment for the exploration of the nurse's work with his or her patient. This is a complicated process that requires support. In my own case, this came from my own manager and supervisor. Having to work something out that was demanding and distressing proved to be a valuable learning experience. The benefits of clinical supervision for nurses have been indicated in nursing literature, but the availability of clinical supervision to nurses demands a high level of commitment from employers in terms of time and training (Kohner, 1994). There have also been calls for further research into the effectiveness of clinical supervision in terms of better nursing care and improvement in patient outcomes in order for NHS trusts to be persuaded into investing in clinical supervision programmes for nurses (White et al., 1998).

The Cassel Hospital is an environment that supports clinical supervision as a useful working tool for nurses. It is a setting where we can examine our professional capabilities and aspects of our personal selves and, as such, is an important aspect of a "culture of enquiry". This can be done without being "analysed". We encourage patients to stick with the distressing, the uncomfortable, and the difficult. This process can lead to change and transformation. We expect them to expose their vulnerabilities and weakness. However, if we are to help them to manage this effectively, then surely we must do this too.

REFERENCES

Armstrong, D. (1991). *The Institution in the Mind*. London: Grubb Institute of Behavioural Studies.

Armstrong, D. (1992). Names, thoughts and lies: the relevance of Bion's late writing for understanding experiences in groups. *Free Associations*, 3: 261–282.

Balint, M. (1957). *The Doctor, His Patient and the Illness*. London: Pitman.

Barker, P. (1992). Psychiatric nursing. In: T. Butterworth & J. Faugier (Eds.), *Clinical Supervision and Mentorship in Nursing*. London: Chapman & Hall.

Barnes, E. (Ed.) (1968). *Psychosocial Nursing: Studies from the Cassel Hospital*. London: Tavistock.

Barnes, E., Griffiths, P., Ord, J., & Wells, D. (Eds.) (1998). *Face to Face with Distress: The Professional Use of Self in Psychosocial Care*. Oxford: Butterworth-Heinemann

Bion, W. R. (1961). *Experiences in Groups*. London: Tavistock.

Brown, A., & Bourne, I. (1996). *The Social Work Supervisor*. Milton Keynes & Philadelphia, PA: Open University Press.

Butterworth, T., & Faugier, J. (Eds.) (1992). *Clinical Supervision and Mentorship in Nursing*. London: Chapman & Hall.

Clark, D. (1964). *Administrative Therapy*. London: Tavistock.

Dartington, A. (1993). Where angels fear to tread. *Winnicott Studies, Vol. 7*, Spring, pp. 21–41.

Denford, J., & Griffiths, P. (1993). Transferences to the institution and their effect on in-patient treatment at the Cassel Hospital. *Therapeutic Communities, 14*: 237–248.

Dept. of Health (1999). *A National Service Framework for Mental Health: Modern Standards and Service Models for Mental Health*. London.

Drahorad, C. (with Frances and Sue) (1999). Reflections on being a patient in a therapeutic community. *Therapeutic Communities, 20* (3).

Eisold, K. (1994). The intolerance of diversity in psychoanalytic institutions. *International Journal of Psycho-Analysis, 75*: 785–800.

Flynn, C. (1993). The patients' pantry: the nature of the nursing task. *Therapeutic Communities, 14*: 227–236.

Flynn, D. (1986). The child's view of the hospital: an examination of the child's experience of an in-patient setting. In: R. Kennedy, A. Heymans, & L. Tischler (Eds.), *The Family as In-Patient* (pp. 208–227). London: Free Association Books.

Flynn, D. (1999). The challenges of in-patient work in a therapeutic community. In: M. Langado & A. Horne (Eds.), *Handbook of Child and Adolescent Psychotherapy: Psychoanalytic Approaches* (pp. 167–182). London: Routledge.

Gabbard, G. (1992). The therapeutic relationship in psychiatric hospital treatment. *Bulletin of the Menninger Clinic, 56* (1): 4–19.

Gabbard, G. (1994). Treatment of borderline patients in a multiple treatment setting. *Psychiatric Clinics of North America, 17* (4): 839–849.

Griffiths, P., & Hinshelwood, R. D. (1997). Actions speak louder than words. In: P. Griffiths & P. Pringle (Eds.), *Psychosocial Practice within a Residential Setting*. Cassel Hospital Monograph Series, No. 1. London: Karnac Books.

Griffiths, P., & Leach, G. (1998). Psychosocial nursing: a model learnt from experience. In: E. Barnes, P. Griffiths, J. Ord, & D. Wells (Eds.), *Face to Face with Distress: The Professional Use of Self in Psychosocial Care*. Oxford: Butterworth-Heinemann.

Griffiths, P., & Pringle, P. (Eds.) (1997). *Psychosocial Practice within a Residential Setting*. Cassel Hospital Monograph Series, No. 1. London: Karnac Books.

Gustafson, J. P. (1976). The pseudomutual small group or institution. *Human Relations, 29*: 989–997.

Halton, W. (1994). Some unconscious aspects of organizational work. In: A. Obholzer & V. Zagier Roberts (Eds.), *The Unconscious at Work* (pp. 11–18). London: Routledge.

Hawkins, P., & Shohet, R. (1989). *Supervision in the Helping Professions.* Milton Keynes: Open University Press.

Hill, J. (1989). Supervision in the caring professions: a literature review. *Community Psychiatric Nursing Journal, 9* (5): 9–15.

Hinshelwood, R. D. (1987). *What Happens in Groups.* London: Free Association Books.

Hinshelwood, R. D., & Skogstad, W. (1998) The hospital in the mind: in-patient psychotherapy at the Cassel Hospital. In: J. Pestalozzi, S. Frisch, R. D. Hinshelwood, & D. Houzel (Eds.), *Psychoanalytic Psychotherapy in Institutional Settings* (pp. 59–73). London: Karnac Books.

James, O. (1986). The role of the nurse/therapist relationship in the therapeutic community. In: R. Kennedy, A. Heymans, & L. Tischler (Eds.), *The Family as In-Patient.* London: Free Association Books.

Janssen, P. L. (1993). The evolution of inpatient psychoanalytic therapy in Germany. *Therapeutic Communities, 14* (4): 265–273.

Janssen, P. L. (1994). *Psychoanalytic Therapy in the Hospital Setting.* London: Routledge.

Joseph, B. (1986). Envy in everyday life. *Psychoanalytical Psychotherapy, 2* (1): 13–22.

Joseph, B. (1989). *Psychic Equilibrium and Psychic Change.* London: Routledge.

Kadushin, A. (1976). *Supervision in Social Work.* New York: Columbia University Press.

Kennedy, R. (1986). Work of the day: aspects of work with families. In: R. Kennedy, A. Heymans, & L. Tischler (Eds.), *The Family as In-Patient* (pp. 27–48). London: Free Association Books.

Kennedy, R. (1997). Working with the work of the day: the use of everyday activities as agents for treatment, change, and transformation. In: P. Griffiths & P. Pringle (Eds.), *Psychosocial Practice within a Residential Setting* (pp. 19–36). Cassel Hospital Monograph Series, No. 1. London: Karnac Books.

Kennedy, R., Heymans, A., & Tischler, L. (1986). *The Family as In-Patient.* London: Free Association Books.

Klein, M. (1935). A contribution to the psychogenesis of manic-depressive states. In: *Love, Guilt and Reparation and Other Works 1921–1945* (pp. 262–289). London: Hogarth Press, 1975.

Kohner, N. (1994). *Clinical Supervision in Practice.* London: Kings Fund Centre.

Main, T. F. (1946). The hospital as a therapeutic institution. In: *The Ailment and Other Psychoanalytic Essays* (pp. 7–11), ed. J. Johns. London: Free Association Books, 1989.

Main, T. F. (1957). The ailment. In: *The Ailment and Other Psychoanalytical Essays*, ed. J. Johns. London: Free Association Books, 1989.

Main, T. F. (1967). Knowledge, learning and freedom from thought. *Australian and New Zealand Journal of Psychiatry*, 1: 64–71.

Main, T. F. (1975a). Psychodynamics of large groups. In: *The Ailment and Other Psychoanalytic Essays* (pp. 100–122), ed. J. Johns. London: Free Association Books, 1989.

Main, T. F. (1975b). Some psychodynamics of large groups. In: L. Kreeger (Ed.), *The Large Group* (pp. 57–86). London: Constable.

Main, T. F. (1983). The concept of a therapeutic community: variations and vicissitudes. In: *The Ailment and Other Psychoanalytic Essays* (pp. 123–141), ed. J. Johns. London: Free Association Books, 1989.

Manning, N. (1979). The politics of survival: the role of research in the therapeutic community. In: R. D. Hinshelwood & N. Manning (Eds.), *Therapeutic Communities: Reflections and Progress*. London: Routledge & Kegan Paul.

Mason, G. (1994). *Cassel Hospital Consumer Evaluation Addendum*. Unpublished, Hammersmith and Fulham Mind.

Meinrath, M., & Roberts, J. (1982). On being a good enough staff member. *International Journal of Therapeutic Communities*, 3: 7–14.

Menzies, I. E. P. (1959). The functioning of social systems as a defence against anxiety. *Human Relations*, 13: 95–121.

Miller, E. J., & Gwynne, G. (1972). *A Life Apart*. London: Tavistock.

Mosse, J. (1994). Introduction: the institutional roots of consulting to institutions. In: A. Obholzer & V. Zagier Roberts (Eds.), *The Unconscious at Work* (pp. 1–10). London: Routledge.

Northcott, N. (1998). The development of guidelines on clinical supervision in clinical practice settings. In: V. Bishop (Ed.), *Clinical Supervision in Practice*. London: Macmillan.

Norton, K. (1992). A culture of enquiry: its preservation or loss. *Therapeutic Communities*, 13: 3–25.

O'Shaughnessy, E. (1992). Enclaves and excursions. *International Journal of Psycho-Analysis, 73*: 603–612.

Pines, M. (Ed.) (1992). *Bion and Group Psychotherapy*. London: Routledge.

Platt-Koch, L. M. (1986). Clinical supervision for psychiatric nurses. *Journal of Psychosocial Nursing, 26* (1): 7–15.

Rapoport, R. N. (1960). *Community as Doctor*. London: Tavistock.

Reed, B. D., & Palmer, B. W. M. (1972). *An Introduction to Organizational Behaviour*. London: Grubb Institute of Behavioural Studies.

Roberts, V. (1994). The self-assigned impossible task. In: A. Obholzer & V. Roberts (Eds.), *The Unconscious at Work*. London: Routledge.

Robinson, S. (1994). Life after death. *Therapeutic Communities, 15*: 77–86.

Rosenfeld, H. A. (1965). *Psychotic States: A Psycho-Analytical Approach*. London: Hogarth Press.

Scanlon, C., & Weir, W. S. (1997). Learning from practice? Mental health nurses' perceptions and experiences of clinical supervision. *Journal of Advanced Nursing, 26*: 295–303.

Simms, J. (1993). The culture of support. In: H. Wright & M. Giddey (Eds.), *Mental Health Nursing: From First Principles to Professional Practice*. London: Chapman & Hall.

Steiner, J. (1993). *Psychic Retreats: Pathological Organizations in Psychotic, Borderline and Neurotic Patients*. London: Routledge.

Stokes, J. (1994). The unconscious at work in groups and teams: contributions from the work of Wilfred Bion. In: A. Obholzer & V. Zagier Roberts (Eds.), *The Unconscious at Work* (pp. 19–27). London: Routledge.

Trist, E., & Murray, H. (Eds.) (1993). *The Social Engagement of Social Science, Vol. 2: The Socio-Technical Perspective*. Philadelphia, PA: University of Pennsylvania Press.

Turquet, P. M. (1985). Leadership: the individual and the group. In: A. D. Colman & M. H. Geller (Eds.), *Group Relations Reader 2*. Washington: A. K. Rice Institute.

UKCC (1996). *Policy Statement on Clinical Supervision for Nursing and Health Visiting*. London: United Kingdom Central Council for Nursing, Midwifery & Health Visiting.

White, E., Butterworth, T., Bishop, V., Carson, J., Jeacock, J., & Clements, A. (1998). Clinical supervision: insider reports of a private world. *Journal of Advanced Nursing, 28* (1): 185–192.

Winnicott, D. W. (1986). *Home Is Where We Start From*. Harmondsworth: Penguin.

Woodhouse, D., & Pengelly, P. (1991). *Anxiety and the Dynamics of Collaboration*. Aberdeen: Aberdeen University Press.

Wright, H. (1989). *Group Work: Perspectives and Practice*. Harrow: Scutari Press.

Wright, H. (1993). The therapeutic relationship. In: H. Wright & M. Giddey (Eds.), *Mental Health Nursing: From First Principles to Professional Practice*. London: Chapman & Hall.

Zagier Roberts, V. (1994). The organization of work: contributions from open systems theory. In: A. Obholzer & V. Zagier Roberts (Eds.), *The Unconscious at Work* (pp. 28–38). London: Routledge.

INDEX